A Saint Squad for Teachers

"Need new perspectives to be inspired by the saints? This is your GEM! Amy Cattapan presents to us a saint squad where we learn and integrate blesseds and saints into our curriculum. Roar with laughter when, like so many of us, Bl. Natalia Tulasiewicz—who loved teaching—refers to grading as 'a nail in the coffin.' Have students who are squirmy? Well, for a few minutes each morning, have them use the 'five finger' method of prayer. Connect history, reading, religion with squad saints who faced social challenges and inequalities. Teaching twins this year? Incorporate some of the anecdotes of Scholastica and Benedict into your lessons to show how twins as well as siblings relate on so many levels to each other. Gift this gem to your faculty right before Christmas as a 'God with us' gift. When tragedy and horror strike, use them to support both faculty and students, reminding the whole school that we are not alone. Moments of sharing from such a powerful resource can keep us all connected and help alleviate the emotional trauma."

Michael McCormack
Theology teacher
St. Thomas Aquinas High School, Fort Lauderdale, FL

"Every teacher would benefit from having a saint squad as coworkers—especially the holy mentors collected in Amy Cattapan's new book, which is filled to the brim with stories of saintly men and women who can inspire us to be the teachers God has created us to be. Whether they are new teachers or veteran catechists, readers will be inspired to follow in the footsteps of this timeless saint squad as they seek to bring young souls closer to Christ."

Katherine Bogner
Catholic school teacher, catechist, and author

"Amy Cattapan's book captures the essence of teaching with the heart. As a high school principal, I plan on integrating these stories into the many reflections we do before prayer at staff meetings. Cattapan's ability to connect the lives of the saints to real, tangible strategies for teachers serves as a guidepost for new educators and a fresh reminder for veterans. For those who strive for authentic, faith-centered relationships with students, this book is a must."

T. K. Griffith
Principal
Archbishop Hoban High School, Akron, Ohio

"This book is a remarkable resource to inspire and form our Catholic schools. Teachers, principals, students, and parents should all find something here to help build Catholic identity."

Tim Uhl
Creator of *Catholic School Matters* podcast and blog
Secretary of Education, Diocese of Buffalo

"Amy Cattapan has provided a gift for Catholic school educators—a book that highlights diverse and fascinating saints who model behaviors that are relevant today. The book includes beautiful, concise stories that are followed with tangible takeaways on key issues that face Catholic schools. Each chapter concludes with reflection questions that make it perfect for a Catholic school book club or a topic for a schoolwide faculty discussion over the course of the year."

Kevin Baxter
Director of the Mary Ann Remick Leadership Program,
Alliance for Catholic Education
Former Superintendent of Schools, Archdiocese of Los Angeles

A Saint Squad for Teachers

45 HEAVENLY FRIENDS TO CARRY YOU THROUGH THE SCHOOL YEAR

AMY J. CATTAPAN

AVE MARIA PRESS AVE Notre Dame, Indiana

Founded in 1865, Ave Maria Press is a ministry of the United States Province of Holy Cross.

www.avemariapress.com

Paperback: ISBN-13 978-1-64680-243-2

E-book: ISBN-13 978-1-64680-244-9

Cover saint images © 2023 Valerie Delgado, paxbeloved.com.

Cover chalkboard image © mallmo / Getty Images.

Cover and text design by Brianna Dombo.

Printed and bound in the United States of America.

Library of Congress Cataloging-in-Publication Data is available.

TO MY FOUR BROTHERS:
DAVE, MIKE, STEVE, AND TOM

THANKS FOR BEING MY ORIGINAL
SQUAD. A GIRL COULDN'T ASK
FOR A BETTER ONE!

Contents

Introduction

> The best preparation for prayer is to read the lives
> of the saints, not from mere curiosity, but quietly
> and with recollection, a little at a time. And to pause
> whenever you feel your heart touched with devotion.
> —St. Philip Neri

Teaching has never been an easy profession. I started teaching high school in the late 1990s, shortly before the Columbine High School shooting. I was teaching middle school on the morning of the 9/11 attacks and when Hurricane Katrina hit. I taught through the COVID-19 pandemic, and I continue to teach as we see more and more school shootings occur.

Is it any wonder that there's a national teacher shortage? In my home state of Illinois, a 2023 study found that 73 percent of schools reported a teacher shortage problem.[1] This is not because there aren't enough qualified teachers out there. A 2022 report by the Economic Policy Institute states what all of us in the profession already know: "The shortage is, instead, a shortfall in the number of qualified teachers *willing to work at current wages and under current working conditions.*"[2] In the last two months, I've learned of three educators within my own network who are leaving the profession entirely. Two left mid-school year, and one is leaving at the end of the year. Two of them have already found higher-paying, less stressful, remote jobs.

While I don't think any of us went into the profession for money, our salary often does not begin to compensate us for the nonstop challenges we face: the constant "on time" with students, having to cover for coworkers because there are never enough subs, larger class sizes due to fewer teachers, angry emails from parents at all hours of the day and night, widespread misconceptions about what teachers actually do—and did I mention the school shootings?

Who could possibly keep teaching under these conditions? What kind of superhumans endure such trials?

Saints. That's who.

And that's right, I'm calling on you and me to walk the path toward sainthood, for only someone on the path to heaven could possibly pick up their cross and carry it daily like a teacher does. The good news? We don't have to walk this path alone. We have mentor saints who have walked this way before us. They have taught in classrooms, served as school leaders, and started new institutions of learning. They did it under great stress, during challenging times, and with little to no monetary compensation.

In recent years, I've often reminded myself of the advice in my first book for teachers, *Sweet Jesus, Is It June Yet?*: Take breaks. It's okay not to be perfect. Allow God's grace to carry you. But many times, I still needed more. I kept picturing that *Star Trek* scene where Captain Kirk asks Scotty for more power, and Scotty says something about giving it all he's got, except in my mind it was me raising my hands to heaven and crying out, "I'm giving it all I've got, Lord. I've got to have more power!"

Thankfully, God put answers right in front of me. Several books about the lives of saints showed up in my life. As I read them, I discovered several things. First, there are many, *many* patron saints of teachers and catechists. Second, in addition to being educators, many saints also started new schools and ushered in reforms in education. Third, even some saints who were not regular classroom teachers provided me with inspiration for my work, either because of their work with children or their relentless pursuit of doing God's will.

Eventually, I built up a little posse of mentor saints. Years ago, it was trendy to post about people you would want on your "team" supporting you with the hashtag #squadgoals. At the time, I was spending my summers in Italy taking courses for my doctorate at Loyola University Chicago's Rome Center and was delighted to discover a number of strong, Italian female saints that could be my "squad" whenever I felt I needed a little extra girl power: St. Catherine of Siena, St. Cecilia, St. Gianna Molla, St. Rita of Cascia, and Bl. Chiara Badano.

Are you in need of your own squad (and #squadgoals)? I have my Italian sisters, but we all need friends who can support us in all areas of our lives. As you read these saints' stories, I pray that it gives you inspiration in your classroom, too—and that you come to think of them as your own "saint squad."

Does the idea of living like a saint seem like a goal too lofty for you? Are you afraid you'll never live up to the example of these canonized saints, or despair of ever being that holy? Don't worry—instead, take comfort in a couple of thoughts.

First, if you were willing to play along with me in the last book and look at Jesus (who is both 100 percent human and 100 percent divine) as a role model, then we really shouldn't be too intimidated by looking at canonized saints (who are 100 percent human and 0 percent divine).

Second, consider that, with the exception of the Blessed Mother, every saint was a sinner. All saint educators made mistakes from time to time. Maybe they occasionally lost their temper, said the wrong thing, or spoke harshly about a colleague who ruffled their feathers. And yet, these all-too-human saintly mentors may inspire you and give you some new strategies for your teacher's toolbox.

For example, St. John Bosco was a creative educator who ran schools for troubled boys in Turin, Italy, at a time when the city was overcrowded, unemployment was high, and many people lived in slums. Later in this book, I'll share some stories about the positive differences he made. However, even St. John Bosco did not succeed in turning his wayward boys into upright citizens 100 percent of the time. Some of his students stole coats, shoes, and bedding. Sometimes they were so loud that it upset their neighbors. And once in a while, St. John Bosco had to remove students from his schools as a last resort. Even a saint can't always set every student on the right path.

So, take heart if you think imitating teacher-saints is going to be impossible. True, we aren't saints just yet (though, *St. Amy* does

A Saint Squad for Teachers

have a nice ring to it). However, our long-term goal is to make it into heaven (whether or not we're officially canonized), and our short-term goal is to find courage, wisdom, and inspiration so that we head into our next school day armed with more grace. In the end, that is all we can ask for.

Let's ask God to send us an abundance of grace, and let's gather together an army of saint friends to inspire us. Many of these holy men and women know the joys and the struggles that teachers face. May reading about them teach us how to follow in their footsteps, and may they intercede for us, asking the Lord to give us the graces we need to be the educators our students need.

All you holy men and women, pray for us!

ONE

Saints Who Used Relatable and Creative Teaching Techniques

How do we reach the poor that they can change their lives? How do we raise up young men and women with the kind of confidence in themselves that says, "I am somebody; I am special"? Even if I am slow, even if I have a drug problem, even if my parents are gone, even if I don't have money, I'm somebody. And there are resources available in my community, and I have to reach out and grab those resources. And I say that of your child, how do we teach the children?
—Servant of God Thea Bowman

How do we teach the children? Isn't that the question educators have been asking themselves for generations? We want to be effective in our work. In *Sweet Jesus, Is It June Yet?*, I shared one educator's observation that "the opportunity to be effective is the single most powerful motivator for entering and staying in teaching and for triggering commitment and effort."[1] However, if we don't know the proper ways to reach (and teach) our students, we won't be effective. That leads to educators leaving the profession.

College courses in methodology and pedagogy are helpful, but sometimes we have to get creative. In this chapter, we look at some holy men and women who went beyond the conventional methods to reach their students and, as a result, had a lasting impact on generations.

Teach Joyfully: Servant of God Thea Bowman

If Thea Bowman (1937–1990) is new to you, you are in for a treat! She is quickly becoming one of my favorite new saint squad members. Although she was a Franciscan Sister of Perpetual Adoration, when asked about her vocation, she didn't say that she was a religious sister. Instead, she replied, "I am a teacher. When I say education, I mean academic education, fiscal education, vocational education, parenting education, moral and value education, cultural education. We need a total educational package, and we need to make it available to everybody."[2]

Born in Yazoo City, Mississippi, to Dr. Theon Bowman and Mary Esther Coleman Bowman, young Bertha was a cherished only child. Her mom taught in public schools for forty-seven years and became principal of the largest African American public elementary school in Greenville, Mississippi.

Bertha began school and Sunday school at age three. She was raised in the Methodist faith of her father; her mother was Episcopalian. Her elders taught her scripture, spirituals, and gospel music as well as the dances and customs of their people. Due to segregation, the public school Bertha attended was poorly funded and understaffed. Dr. and Mrs. Bowman knew their daughter was bright and not being challenged, so when the Franciscan Sisters of Perpetual Adoration from La Crosse, Wisconsin, were asked to start the Holy Child Jesus Mission School in Canton, the Bowmans jumped at the chance to enroll their daughter in the charter sixth-grade class.

Young Bertha was immediately attracted to the joyful priests and sisters at Holy Child Jesus Mission School. She decided on her own to convert to Catholicism and at age fifteen went on a hunger strike to compel her parents to grant her permission to enter the order as an aspirant. Eventually they consented, and Bertha was sent to St. Rose Convent School in La Crosse. Her arrival in La Crosse became a news story since she was the first Black woman to try to enter the order. Despite facing discrimination and prejudice, she won over many of the sisters with her joy and love for Christ.

In 1955, Bertha began her studies at Viterbo College, and a year later she entered the novitiate and became Sr. Thea. Her academic brilliance convinced her superiors she would make a great educator, so in 1959 she received her first assignment: teaching fifth and sixth grade at Blessed Sacrament School in La Crosse. This caused a bit of a stir at the all-white school. The principal wisely invited the parents to a session where they could meet Sr. Thea, who quickly delighted them with her Southern charm, joy, and warmth.

After two years at Blessed Sacrament, Sr. Thea got the teaching position she had hoped for. She was sent back to teach at her alma mater, Holy Child Jesus Mission School. She began at the elementary level again but was later moved to teaching high school, where she found the boys' lack of interest in reading to be very challenging. When she discovered they loved comics, she gave them writing assignments about the characters in comic strips and used this as an entryway to get them interested in books.

Sr. Thea had tremendous success in teaching her students music. Within a few years, her fifty-member school choir was ready to record an album of African American spirituals. In fact, incorporating music into her lessons became a hallmark of Sr. Thea's calling as both an educator and a speaker. She was known to break into song in the middle of her presentations and encourage her students and audience members to sing along.

A lifelong learner, Sr. Thea earned both master's and doctoral degrees in English from the Catholic University of America. In 1972, she became a professor at Viterbo College before returning home to Canton in 1978 to take care of her aging parents. At this time, she also became the director for intercultural affairs in the Diocese of Jackson and a founding faculty member of the Institute for Black Catholic Studies at Xavier University of Louisiana.

In 1984, both of Sr. Thea's parents died, and she was diagnosed with breast cancer. She continued her teaching and speaking as much as she could, inspiring her students and those who were blessed to hear her. On June 17, 1989, she gave a speech to the US Catholic bishops at their annual meeting, during which she got them all to sing "We Shall Overcome," and shared with them this important message:

> What does it mean to be Black and Catholic? It means that I come to my church fully functioning. That doesn't frighten you, does it? I come to my church fully functioning. I bring myself, my Black self, all that I am, all that I have, all that I hope to become, I bring my whole history, my traditions, my experience, my culture, my African-American song and dance and gesture and movement and teaching and preaching and healing and responsibility as gift to the church.[3]

WHAT CAN WE LEARN FROM SERVANT OF GOD THEA BOWMAN?

The quality of Sr. Thea Bowman that I most admire is her joy. If you've never seen video footage of her, watch her 1989 talk to the US Catholic bishops. She gave this talk about five years into her battle with cancer and only one year before her death. Oh, Lord, teach me to have such passion and joy for my work!

When I look at the story of Sr. Thea's life, there are a couple of other lessons that resonate with me as well.

- *You don't need to be a music teacher to add music to your classroom.* A principal once shared with me how he had stepped into one of my younger colleagues' classrooms and loved how she incorporated music into her math lesson. Well, I immediately had to find out more about that! What I learned completely changed the way I design my lessons. This lovely coworker showed me how to put all my lessons onto Google Slides and then embed musical timers from YouTube into the slides. I cannot tell you how this simple change has revolutionized my lessons.

   Do I want my students to have their bell-ringer activity completed in just a minute or two? Then I find a fun music timer with the appropriate length and insert it into the slide with the instructions. Do I want my students to calm down and settle into a writing assignment? Then I pick a long timer with lo-fi study music. While my students might laugh at some of my musical choices (laughter is inevitable in middle school), they often enjoy the selections, and I get requests to repeat certain ones! It's a quick, simple way to add a little fun to our day, and the timer aspect motivates students to finish on time.

- *Remember that your students bring "their whole selves" to class.* Sr. Thea Bowman implored the bishops to remember that she brought her whole self to the Church. That's why, in later years, she eschewed the conventional religious sister's habit for more traditional African clothes. She didn't want to hide any part of who she was because who she was, was a gift to the Church.

Our students are a gift to us. Like Sr. Thea, they bring their culture, traditions, languages, songs, and more into our schools. Do we recognize all they bring as gifts? In the wake of George Floyd's death, I heard some beautiful and important conversations played out on various Catholic podcasts. People talked about looking at the artwork in Catholic churches and schools. Were saints of all colors depicted? Was the Holy Family always portrayed as fair-skinned and European? Were demons invariably dark-skinned? If we're truly allowing our students to bring all that they are to our classrooms, then we need to make sure there are opportunities for them to see their cultures and their languages represented in our artwork, our literature, and all aspects of our curricula.

Embrace Culturally Relevant Teaching: Servant of God Antonio Cuipa

One of the eighty-six Martyrs of La Florida, Antonio Cuipa was born to a Christian Apalachee family in the seventeenth century. Educated by the Franciscans who had converted his parents, Antonio grew up in San Luis de Talimali, a large Spanish mission, and became a leader in his community. He married a Christian woman, and they had two children.

As an adult, Antonio often went with the Franciscans to non-Christian tribes to translate for them and to preach. Wherever he went to teach the Gospel, he began by playing the flute. His extraordinary musical talent easily won their admiration, and he also gave out hand-carved flutes and maize cakes as gifts. Only then did he begin to tell them about God's love for them.

Antonio explained that the creator God they knew had a Son named Jesus, who became man and died to save them. Antonio was so successful and well respected that he became an *inija* ("noble leader"), second only to the chief of the Apalachee. He and his converts from the San Luis mission were martyred trying to defend the neighboring La Concepción de Ayubale mission from an attack by English troops and Creek Indian mercenaries.[4]

WHAT CAN WE LEARN FROM SERVANT OF GOD ANTONIO CUIPA?

The subject of my dissertation was using culturally relevant literature in the classroom. If I had known of Servant of God Antonio Cuipa and his use of culturally relevant pedagogy to spread the faith, he would have been on my saint squad much sooner, and I definitely would have asked his intercession as I barreled my way through my research. Here are some important tips I learned from him.

- *Use relatable art in your lessons.* I love that Antonio Cuipa connected with his listeners and built trust by using culturally relevant music to capture their attention and to let them know he understood where they were coming from. Both Sr. Thea Bowman and Antonio Cuipa used music related to their culture when teaching. How do you use various forms of art (music, paintings, sculpture, architecture, dance) to connect with your students?
- *Start with what they already know.* Antonio saw connections between what the tribes already believed and what he had learned as a Christian. He knew that the way "in" was to affirm what they already knew—that they were created by a God who loved them. Then he built on that shared belief by telling them that the creator God they already knew had a Son, and this Son meant good news for all of us. As educators, we know that we learn when our brain makes connections between the new information we are perceiving and old information already stored in our minds. Antonio Cuipa didn't know the brain science behind what he was doing, but he instinctively used prior knowledge as a way to help his students learn their catechism.

Repurpose Pop Culture: St. Ephrem the Syrian

St. Ephrem the Syrian (306–373) has been nicknamed the "Harp of the Holy Spirit" for the way he used music as a means of teaching. (Hmm, I'm sensing a theme.) During the fourth century, heretics were using songs to spread false teachings. He decided to use their own method to combat their efforts. He even took some of the same tunes and rewrote the songs; often the Christian hymns outlasted the original lyrics.

Ephrem also composed his own songs, wrote poetry, and delivered riveting homilies that moved people to tears. His poetry, in particular, was known for its empathy for people experiencing pain. From these poems, he composed at least eighty-five funeral hymns.

As an educator, Ephrem spent twenty-five years in charge of a school in Nisibis, Syria. However, when the Persians took over Nisibis in 350, Ephrem fled to the mountains near Edessa, where he lived in a cave. From there, he made periodic excursions to the city to preach, where he continued to win over people with his powerful words.

WHAT CAN WE LEARN FROM ST. EPHREM THE SYRIAN?

I once heard a speaker say that even seemingly unmotivated students are capable of learning. He gave examples of students who didn't seem interested in learning math or science but would spend hours watching tutorials on YouTube about how to get to the next level of their favorite video game. When Minecraft was popular with my nephews, my brothers and sisters-in-law were surprised at how much their boys learned about obsidian and basalt because they wanted to use them in their Minecraft creations. If students are motivated to learn, they will find a way to do so. Are we paying attention to what they are already learning and how they are learning it?

- *Adopt methods that are already working.* Ephrem saw that heretics were successfully spreading their messages with popular songs, and he figured that the best way to beat them was to join their game. When I realized how much young people use YouTube, I decided to start incorporating more videos, like BrainPop and Khan Academy, into my lessons. At first, I think my own ego held me back from using these resources. Shouldn't my kids just listen to me instead?

  But then I realized what St. Ephrem realized: Why fight it? If it's working, use it! And to be honest, I really enjoy using short videos in my class. It breaks up the lessons. I can offer a mini-lesson on a grammar topic one day, and then use a brief online video at the start of the next day to review. Don't we all hate repeating ourselves anyway? And if there are a few children in the room who will pay more attention to a video than to the teacher standing in front of them, so be it! Sometimes, tutorial videos say things slightly differently than I do or provide different examples that might click with some students better than my own words or examples.

- *Incorporate games into your lesson plans.* You're probably familiar with at least one of the following: Kahoot!, Quizlet, Quizizz, Blooket, or Gimkit. What do they have in common? They use elements of the video games our students can't get enough of to create review games for students. As a middle-aged woman, I don't understand the huge excitement over "power-ups" and "superplays," but if it makes my students excited about practicing their vocabulary words or grammar rules, then count me in!

Make Learning Fun: St. Philip Neri

Philip Neri (1515–1595) was born the youngest son of a noble family in Florence. Apprenticed to a wealthy uncle, at age eighteen Philip had a strong religious experience that induced him to move to Rome to study. He lived in poverty but became a tutor to support himself.

As he studied, Philip took to the streets to evangelize. On his daily walks around Rome, he talked with people to strengthen their faith. Often young people would join him on his little "pilgrimages" around town, and he would joke, sing, and pray with them.

In 1551, Philip was ordained a priest. Later, he organized a small group of priests into the Congregation of the Oratory, a community that held conferences for study and prayer. These usually ended in music or a short pilgrimage to an ancient basilica. Whether his students were young or old, rich or poor, or even the pope himself, Philip used kindness and humor to instruct and evangelize. For his work, he has been called the "Second Apostle of Rome."[5]

WHAT CAN WE LEARN FROM ST. PHILIP NERI?

St. Philip Neri reminds us that not all learning happens in the classroom—and that our own disposition as teachers can enhance our students' ability to learn.

- *Don't underestimate the power of humor.* In high school I joined the drama club, where I did some improv exercises. I hated them at the time. Just give me a script with lines to memorize. However, early in my teaching career I learned that my "script" for each day never goes exactly as planned. The ability to think on my feet (thanks to improv) helped me to adapt lessons and answer unexpected questions appropriately. In other words, teaching has really improved my improv and stand-up comic skills—and these skills in turn have helped me hold my students' attention.

In addition, humor is a powerful connecting tool. When we laugh with someone, we bond through a shared experience. Letting students see that we have a sense of humor helps them view us as regular people who care about them and want to enjoy a laugh with them every now and then.

- *Take field trips (even short and virtual ones).* I smile when I picture Philip Neri walking around Rome taking his students on short pilgrimages to the many basilicas there. When I studied for my doctorate at Loyola University Chicago, I took three of my elective courses at the Rome Center. For each class, the instructors brought us to different sites. I had classes in the Jesuit Refugee Service, the Colosseum, the Roman Forum, outside (and inside!) churches such as San Clemente and Santa Maria del Popolo, and even in the rooms of St. Ignatius, where he wrote and lived during the final years of his life.

Years ago, one of my coworkers reminded me that some of our students' parents might never take them to a museum or a play. Our field trips might be their first time visiting such places. What a privilege to be there with them! Sure, organizing field trips is a ton of work, but you can reap many rewards—some you might not even know about unless you ask! Have your students write an evaluation of the field trip after you return: What did they like about it? What did they not like? And what's one thing they learned or one thing that surprised them?

Remember Maslow's Hierarchy: St. Peter Claver

Originally from Catalonia, Spain, Peter Claver (1580–1654) entered the Jesuit novitiate at the age of twenty and was sent to the Jesuit school in Palma. There he met the lay brother Alphonsus Rodriguez, who became his spiritual director and who had a revelation that Peter would be sent away to care for enslaved people.

In 1610, Peter was sent to Cartagena, in modern-day Colombia, to do precisely what Alphonsus had predicted. He took with him notebooks filled with guidance from his spiritual director. When he arrived in Cartagena, he assisted Fr. Alphonsus de Sandoval, a fellow Jesuit, who ministered to enslaved Africans.

When ships arrived in Cartagena, Fr. Alphonsus and Peter would climb down into the holds where the captive men and women waited to be sold; they were hungry, thirsty, and often diseased. Together the men cleaned the people's wounds and tried to comfort them, bringing them familiar foods such as sweet potatoes, oranges, lemons, and bananas.

For forty years, Peter Claver fed, bathed, and tended to the needs of hundreds of thousands of people who passed through this center of the slave trade. Peter and Fr. Alphonsus also preached to the enslaved, but only after caring for their physical needs. Peter Claver explained, "We must speak to them with our hands before we try to teach them with our lips."[6]

To respect each person's dignity, Peter Claver separated the men and women for privacy and brought clothes to cover them. If he didn't have clothes with him at the time, he laid his cloak over the individual he was tending to. Despite the cloak being soiled from the sick people's ulcers, it released a beautiful perfume.

Peter knew a bit of some of the African languages, but he often used pictures and interpreters to help him teach Christianity. After working all day, he spent his nights in penance and prayer. As best he could, he followed up with those he baptized, estimated to be more than three hundred thousand people. He visited plantations, hospitals, and mines to check on the new Christians, always staying with them instead of accepting any lodgings offered by the slave owners. When he made his final profession, he signed the document, "Peter Claver, slave of the Africans."[7]

WHAT CAN WE LEARN FROM ST. PETER CLAVER?

Remember Maslow's "hierarchy of needs"? It's such a basic thing, but so important for us to remember. Our students' physical needs must be met before they can learn. Peter Claver knew this instinctively hundreds of years before Maslow created his famous hierarchy with self-actualization at the top and physiological needs at the bottom.

- *Recognize physical needs first.* Before he preached to the enslaved people, Peter took care of their sores, their hunger, and their illnesses. Reading about how he put their physical needs first reminded me of my high school German teacher. One day, a student in our class fell asleep with only a few minutes left in the period. We were a small, close-knit group, and we quietly informed our beloved German teacher that the boy was asleep. She waved a hand dismissively. "Let him sleep," she said. "He worked the late shift at the gas station last night. The poor boy needs his rest." At that moment, she realized he needed rest more than he needed a few minutes of reviewing German verbs.
- *Create a space of love and belonging.* Peter Claver not only brought the enslaved people food but did his best to find foods that would be familiar and a comfort to them. He treated the enslaved with respect and dignity because, as Maslow pointed out, after physiological needs are met, we need to feel a sense of love and belonging. Consider the ways you create a sense of community in your classroom (more on this in the next chapter). How might Peter Claver inspire you?

Saint Squad Summary: One Size Doesn't Fit All

God has a way of delighting me with answers to questions I didn't know I had. As I was working on this chapter, I started listening to

Fr. Mike Schmitz's *Catechism in a Year* podcast, and I was struck by something in the prologue. It's actually a quote from the preface to the *Roman Catechism*:

> Whoever teaches must become "all things to all men" (1 Cor 9:22), to win everyone to Christ. . . . Above all, teachers must not imagine that a single kind of soul has been entrusted to them, and that consequently it is lawful to teach and form equally all in the faithful in true piety with one and the same method! Let them realize that some are in Christ as newborn babes, others as adolescents, and still others as adults in full command of their powers. . . . Those who are called to the ministry of preaching must suit their words to the maturity and understanding of their hearers.[8]

As teachers, we've been entrusted with many kinds of souls, not just one. No single teaching method will help us reach all of our students. As a visual learner, I probably leaned heavily on visual methods of learning in my early years of teaching, but as I've persevered, I've opened up to various other types of learning, adding in more opportunities for group and partner sharing, more short videos and music, more games, and more kinesthetic activities.

The saints in this chapter used music, art, humor, field trips, and more to help students learn. May they inspire us to get creative in our teaching methods and try new things so that we can become "all things to all students," even if it means stepping outside our comfort zones.

REFLECTION QUESTIONS

1. Sr. Thea Bowman and St. Philip Neri were known for their joyful and infectious personalities. How can you bring joy into your classroom? Can you make your students' cultural diversity an integral part of your lessons?

2. Servant of God Antonio Cuipa used music as part of his preaching. How can you use art or music to start your lessons so that students make connections between what they already know and what you want them to learn?

3. St. Ephrem the Syrian adapted popular songs and turned them into teaching tools. How can you adapt things your students already enjoy so that they fit your curriculum?

4. St. Peter Claver knew that basic needs have to be met before learning can occur. When have you had to help students with needs at the bottom of Maslow's hierarchy?

TWO

Saints Who Built Strong Relationships

Eternal God, I pray to you, for all those you have given me to love with a special love, and with special concern. Let them be illumined with your light. Let all imperfection be taken from them, so that in truth they may work in your garden, where you have assigned them to work.

—from St. Catherine of Siena's
"Prayer for Her Friends"

I don't remember exactly when I started praying daily for my students, but it began shortly after Pope Francis was elected, and he talked about his morning "Five Finger Prayer." On your thumb, the finger closest to your body, you pray for those closest to you, your family and friends. On your pointer finger, you pray for those who instruct you (like teachers!). On your middle finger (the tallest one), you pray for the leaders of the world. On your ring finger (the weakest one), you pray for those who are sick or suffering. Finally, on your pinkie, you pray for your own needs.

I decided to try it. Praying for family and friends was easy, but what to do about the pointer finger? I was in between my master's degree and my doctorate, so I didn't have any teachers at the time. No problem! I decided to pray for my students instead. Later, I decided to add my coworkers. Eventually, I added my administrators. As I type this, I'm realizing I should probably add my students' parents to the list as well!

Think about all the different relationships required of us as teachers. Students aren't the only ones with whom we need to maintain good relationships. Despite the solitary nature of our jobs, it's really a team effort. We have to work in conjunction with our colleagues, administrators, and parents in order to best reach these young minds entrusted to us.

Let's see how saints who were effective teachers and preachers created and maintained strong relationships.

Cultivate Trust: St. Catherine of Siena

St. Catherine of Siena (1347–1380) was never a regular classroom teacher, but I'm including her for a few reasons. First, she is a Doctor of the Church, one of the great teachers of the faith, mostly because of what she wrote in nearly four hundred surviving letters. Second, she is remembered as a great preacher, though the idea of a woman preaching about the faith would have seemed preposterous in the fourteenth century. And finally, I retroactively adopted her as my Confirmation saint years ago, and I'm pretty sure she would be giving me that "teacher look" if I didn't include her here.

In all seriousness, I love many things about St. Catherine. Like me, she was kind of a tough little Italian woman who was a lay member of a religious order (Catherine was a Third Order Dominican; I am a Dame of the Order of Malta). When she thought the pope, civil leaders, priests, or anyone else was doing something wrong, she was not afraid to tell them to straighten up and do their job!

You might think that, back in the fourteenth century, men would have ignored a woman's advice. However, they didn't ignore Catherine. Despite her sometimes strongly worded reprimands (she once told Pope Gregory XI to "be a courageous man for me, not a coward"),[1] these men saw her as a friend and a loving mother, someone who could be trusted. In fact, after she persuaded Pope Gregory XI to return to Rome (after having spent years in Avignon, France), he trusted her so much that he sent her as his ambassador to Florence to ensure peace in that area.

At that time, Italy was a collection of city-states, not a unified country. There was also no separation between church and state. This meant that there were often disagreements and wars between cities. Catherine worked for peace, sending letters encouraging all in civil and religious positions of authority to put down their weapons and negotiate.

Like many other saints in this book, Catherine also worked tirelessly for the poor. Her way of living out her faith was so appealing that she attracted her own followers, the Caterinata, who worked with her to care for the poor in Siena. They lived in poverty themselves, baking bread and begging for alms to feed their neighbors. So devoted were they to St. Catherine that they referred to her as "Mamma." One of these women was her dear friend Alessa, who was Catherine's constant companion until her death.

The key to Catherine's success was her ability to develop strong relationships, often with the most unlikely people. For example, her confessor, Raymond of Capua, was much older, well educated, and experienced, but even he found himself listening intently to young, unschooled Catherine. Because she was most likely illiterate until the final years of her life, she dictated many of her letters to Raymond, who came to regard her as a sort of spiritual mother. They spent a great deal of time together, and he was deeply saddened to have been absent at her death because the pope had sent him on an errand. After Catherine died, Raymond wrote the first biography of her, in which he stated that everyone who met her "rejoiced with a new sort of joy."[2]

WHAT CAN WE LEARN FROM ST. CATHERINE OF SIENA?

St. Catherine cared so much for her friends, followers, and neighbors that she often made extreme sacrifices in supplication to God to save their souls. Before beginning her ministry, she spent years alone in her room, eating little except the Eucharist and sleeping on a board. I don't really see myself doing that any time soon. ("Hangry" is not a good way to face a classroom of middle schoolers!) However, there are ways I can still imitate her holiness in my work as an educator.

- *Don't be afraid of the higher-ups.* (And if you are a higher-up, don't be afraid to listen to those "below" you!) Catherine firmly believed that the work she was doing was God's work. She had experienced a mystical union with Christ in which she saw Christ slip an invisible wedding band onto her finger. With that kind of conviction, no wonder she didn't fear telling the pope himself to man up and get back to Rome!

  Those of us who are classroom educators might fear telling our administrators what we really think, but if we truly believe we are doing God's work (and thus, have the students' best interests in mind), then we shouldn't let our fears keep us from speaking up for our students. Note the way Catherine wrote to civil and religious leaders. Sure, she could word things very strongly, but those critiques and reprimands were counterbalanced with words of affirmation and encouragement. It's taken me a long time in my career to feel like I'm in a place where I can speak my mind with my administrators but also lift them up with my support.

- *Consider your position as a parental figure.* St. Catherine was a lay Dominican. She was not a religious sister, but she also never married or had kids. Yet she looked after her followers as if they were her own children, and they called her "Mamma." Clearly, she had created a family atmosphere, and my best school years have always been ones where my students and I have bonded in a similar way.

Keep Close to Your Sheep: St. Antoninus

Born in Florence, Antoninus (1389–1459) was nicknamed "Little Antony" for his diminutive height. As a teenager, he asked to enter the Dominican house in nearby Fiesole. To test his sincerity, the superior told him to memorize the book of the Decretals, which is hundreds of pages long. Antoninus did it in twelve months and entered the Dominican house at age sixteen.

Most of Antoninus's teachings can be found in his major four-volume work *Summa Theologica Moralis*, which was published in 1477 and went through fifteen editions in its first fifty years. In this work, Antoninus taught that humans have inherent dignity because they are made in God's image.

Although he ascended to the position of archbishop of Florence, which he held from 1446 to 1459, Antoninus insisted on living a simple life. He did not own a single plate or a horse. He had one mule, which he sold to feed the poor, but every time he sold it, a benefactor would buy it back for him. He dug up flowers and planted wheat to feed the hungry. He lived in the archbishop's palace but sold his furniture and clothing so he could provide for those in need. He established a benefit society to help those who were ashamed to ask for assistance.

Antoninus believed pastors needed to model themselves after Christ the Good Shepherd and lead by example. He visited every parish in his diocese on foot once a year so that he could hear the concerns of everyone. He loved his people and they loved him, though he could be strict. He once threw some young men out of church for spending too much time looking at the young women present.

Antoninus was known as the "Counsellor" because so many people wanted his prudent advice. He was also known as the "Father of the Poor" because whenever he asked someone for alms for the poor, he was not refused.

WHAT CAN WE LEARN FROM ST. ANTONINUS?

Administrators might relate to St. Antoninus more than classroom teachers since he spent years as an archbishop, but his advice for pastors is good for both principals and teachers.

- *Model yourself after the Good Shepherd.* Jesus is the Good Shepherd because he cares for us in a loving and protective way. As teachers, do we see ourselves in the role of shepherds? Ours is not an easy task. Sometimes it means caring for and protecting children; other times being a teacher means being firm. Consider how a shepherd sometimes uses his crook to bring back a wandering sheep. It's not a painful action but rather a firm nudge to get back in line. At the same time, Jesus tells us that shepherds will go out of their way to bring back one sheep that is lost (see Luke 15:3–7). Are we willing to go out of our way to bring back that one student who has wandered away?

- *Visit your people.* This teaching can be interpreted several ways. First of all, as a classroom teacher, I make various efforts to check in with my students one-on-one. Depending on the year and my schedule, this might mean individual writing conferences, if my classes are small. If I'm teaching many students, it might mean focusing my efforts on my advisory group or my study hall and doing weekly grade check-ins with them.

  For those who are administrators, St. Antoninus might remind you of the importance of visiting the classrooms in your school, and not just at teacher evaluation time! As a classroom teacher, I welcome administrators into my room whenever they want to pop in, and in recent years I've begun to pull them into the lesson as well. I think it's important that the kids don't just see the principal or the assistant principal as the person they are sent to if they get into trouble.

  Pulling an administrator into the lesson doesn't have to be complicated, either. I start my classes with a warm-up activity, such as an entrance slip, a quick question of the day, or a four-minute freewrite. If an administrator comes in during this time, I invite them to answer our question of the day or share how they might respond to the freewriting prompt. In my early teaching years, I probably would have thought this was a waste of time, but I've grown to love it. It's fun to hear what the administrators say, and they enjoy hearing the kids' responses, too. It builds a sense of community that helps the students know that all of us in the building are on the same page.

Ask God for Help: Benedict and Scholastica, Sibling Saints

The founder of the Benedictines, St. Benedict of Nursia (480–547) is often called the father of Western monasticism. But did you know he had a twin? What we know about his sister, St. Scholastica (480–543), comes mostly from St. Gregory the Great. Scholastica consecrated herself to God as a child and entered religious life at a young age.

As a young man, Benedict studied in Rome, but he grew discouraged by the immoral behavior of those around him and left. He became a hermit who lived in a rocky cave near Subiaco, Italy, and ended up gaining followers, whom he later divided into twelve communities and taught for twenty years. As the Roman Empire began to fall, he established monasteries throughout Europe, including the famous Monte Cassino, which became a center of Christian worship and learning. Scholastica founded the feminine branch of the Benedictines at a convent five miles south of Monte Cassino.

The twins were known for being close but (like many siblings) also competitive. Because of the strict rules Benedict had established for his order, he only met with his sister once a year at a cave between their communities. At these meetings they would discuss spiritual matters and pray together.

According to St. Gregory's account, the last time Benedict and Scholastica met, she asked him to stay longer. Benedict refused because of the strict curfew he had set up for his own order. Determined not to let their visit end, Scholastica prayed, and immediately a terrible thunderstorm began, making it impossible for Benedict to return home. "May almighty God spare you, sister. What have you done?" he reprimanded her.

"I asked you, but you were unwilling to listen to me," she replied. "I asked my Lord and he listened to me."[3]

They spent the remainder of the night talking and praying. Three days later, St. Scholastica died. Benedict saw her soul rising to heaven as a dove and had her body laid to rest in a tomb that had been prepared for himself.

WHAT CAN WE LEARN FROM ST. BENEDICT AND ST. SCHOLASTICA?

I love this story of two sibling saints who shared conversations about faith because it reminds me of my relationship with my four brothers. Despite enjoying our conversations together, we don't always agree. Perhaps you feel the same way about discussing teaching with some of your colleagues.

- *Ask God to strengthen even your good relationships.* Benedict and Scholastica enjoyed their yearly meetings, but they disagreed about what time to wrap up their discussions. When she needed help convincing her brother, Scholastica prayed to God—and he provided a rainstorm! Think about those colleagues you normally agree with. Do you sometimes disagree? In those cases, ask God for a little extra grace, just as Scholastica asked for a little extra time.
- *Make sure that your classroom rules and procedures support your mission.* On the day of their last conversation together, Benedict wanted to follow the strict rules of his monastery and return home that evening. Scholastica needed more time to discuss the faith with her brother. It was so important to her that she asked him to bend his own order's rules. Consider whether your

classroom rules provide you with the flexibility necessary to meet the needs of your students.

Have a Good Network:
St. Marie-Eugénie de Jésus

Anne-Eugénie Milleret de Brou (1817–1898), later Sr. Marie-Eugénie de Jésus and the patron saint of educators and students, was born in Metz, France, to wealthy parents who were what we might call "culturally Catholic." Simply put, the family was more interested in politics than in their faith. However, when Anne-Eugénie received her first Communion at age twelve, she had a strong spiritual experience that forever changed her.

As she left the communion rail and looked at the sea of people in the pews, Anne-Eugénie began to panic that she would not find her mother. Suddenly, a voice inside her said, "You will lose your mother, but I shall be for you more than a mother. A day will come when you will leave everything you love in order to glorify me and serve this church that you do not know."[4] A year later, her father became bankrupt, and her parents separated. Anne-Eugénie went with her mother to Paris. Two years later, her mother died of cholera.

The following Lent, Anne-Eugénie went to the Cathedral of Notre Dame to hear a famous preacher, and she felt called to give her life to God. She wrote to this preacher for advice, and he told her to be patient, pray, and read. The next year, she met Fr. Théodore Combalot, who introduced her to Fr. Emmanuel d'Alzon. Fr. d'Alzon would play an important role in her life and become one of her closest friends.

In 1839, Anne-Eugénie, now Sr. Marie-Eugénie de Jésus, cofounded an educational order, the Religious of the Assumption, with Fr. Combalot. Meanwhile, she encouraged Fr. d'Alzon to open a counterpart to her order for men, which would be called the Augustinians of the Assumption. Fr. d'Alzon and Sr. Marie-Eugénie helped each other pursue holiness even though they lived five hundred miles apart. Their friendship lasted almost forty years, until the priest's death. Although they didn't always agree, Marie-Eugénie stated after his passing, "I have made it a habit to see in people only what I shall see for all eternity. What I shall see eternally in Fr. d'Alzon is his love for Jesus Christ, his devotion to the Church, his zeal for souls."[5]

Sr. Marie-Eugénie's other close friend was Kate O'Neill, a young Irish woman who had emigrated to France with her sister. After the two young women heard Fr. Théodore Combalot preach, Kate decided to talk with him about becoming a religious sister. Fr. Combalot's persuasive skills convinced her to join the Religious of the Assumption, and she became Sr. Thérèse Emmanuel, the mistress of novices until her death in 1888.

The two friends had very different temperaments and cultural backgrounds, and had their share of disagreements. Sr. Thérèse Emmanuel also had mystical experiences that Marie-Eugénie didn't always know how to interpret. Nonetheless, when push came to shove, they had each other's backs. Whenever there was a threat to the unity of the Assumption (such as when Fr. Combalot tried to separate Marie-Eugénie from the rest of the order), Sr. Thérèse Emmanuel supported Marie-Eugénie's authority as the superior and her decision to keep them together. When some sisters were needed to care for orphans in another city, Marie-Eugénie sent Thérèse Emmanuel, referring to her as her "good right arm."[6]

WHAT CAN WE LEARN FROM ST. MARIE-EUGÉNIE DE JÉSUS?

St. Marie-Eugénie dedicated her life to the education of girls and the poor, but the order of sisters she cofounded couldn't have happened without her network of friends.

- *You don't have to get along perfectly to have each other's backs.* Marie-Eugénie de Jésus was supported by her priest and religious sister friends. Even though they disagreed at times about how the order should be run and where it should operate, they still assisted each other. There will be times when we do not agree with what our coworkers say. When that happens, it might be helpful to take St. Marie-Eugénie's approach and think of them in the same way we hope to see them for all eternity (as deeply devoted educators dedicated to the same cause).

- *Choose educator friends who will inspire you.* Thinking the best of people and having their back doesn't mean you have to be work buddies with someone whose attitude has a negative effect on you. Although Fr. Théodore Combalot was instrumental at the start of the new congregation, Sr. Marie-Eugénie found herself turning more and more to Fr. Emmanuel d'Alzon for mutual support. We need work friends who will challenge us to be our best and lift us up when we need a boost.

Saint Squad Summary: Be Authentic, Be Humble

Consider ways that being authentic and humble can help you in your relationships with your students, your coworkers, and your students' parents. As a beginning teacher, I struggled with how much of myself to share with my students. Certainly, we don't need to overshare all the personal details, but letting our students know that we are real humans with real emotions, likes, and dislikes can make us much more relatable.

Years ago, when I was teaching sixth and seventh grade at a Catholic school, I had to cover a fifth-grade indoor recess duty. I'd been warned there were some tough boys who played rather rough at recess. They were bright students who did well during lessons but often got in trouble on the playground. I braced myself for twenty minutes of terror with the "bad boys" as they were stuck inside on a rainy day. However, during that twenty minutes, I spotted a copy of *The Lord of the Rings* on a desk. At the time, one of the movies had just hit theaters, and I said something about it.

"Wait!" said one of the ringleaders. "You've seen *The Lord of the Rings* movies?"

"Yes." Quite frankly, I was shocked that he was shocked.

"I didn't know teachers watched *cool* movies," he replied.

It was the beginning of building a positive relationship with him, and I thank God I had that small opportunity for interaction before those boys even stepped foot in my sixth-grade classroom.

Consider how the saints in this chapter built strong, positive relationships. St. Catherine told it like it was when reprimanding warring factions. St. Antoninus held high standards while living a simple, humble life. St. Scholastica and St. Benedict were competitive in a way that incorporated the best kind of peer pressure. And St. Marie-Eugénie and her friends supported each other even when they disagreed. Being authentic and being humble are building blocks to holy and helpful relationships.

REFLECTION QUESTIONS

1. People of all social ranks listened to St. Catherine of Siena because they trusted her. How do you build strong relationships with your students, coworkers, and administrators?

2. St. Antoninus visited the people under his care often. How do you find ways to check in with your students (or staff, if you're an administrator) that are personal and not purely evaluative?

3. St. Scholastica asked St. Benedict to bend his rules so they could continue to discuss the faith. How do your classroom rules bend to meet the needs of your students?

4. St. Marie-Eugénie forged lifelong friendships with people who helped her in her ministry. Where have you found educator friends (at your own school or beyond) who inspire and support you?

THREE

Saints Who Dealt with Challenging Students

Do you have these sentiments of charity and tenderness toward the poor children whom you have to educate? If you have for them the firmness of a father to restrain and withdraw them from misbehavior, you must also have for them the tenderness of a mother to draw them to you, and to do for them all the good that depends on you.

—St. Jean-Baptiste de La Salle

One area of education in which I've never felt 100 percent comfortable is teaching students who might be considered "challenging." I'm not talking about general classroom management (although that certainly worried me early in my career); I'm talking about the many ways students test our limits.

Some students are challenging because of unmet needs, such as those who seek extra attention or require extra assistance due to an unidentifiable (or yet-to-be-diagnosed) learning disability. Others are on the opposite end of the spectrum, such as those in honors courses who are either bored or suffer from perfectionism and anxiety.

In *Sweet Jesus, Is It June Yet?*, I talked about how some students are like the tax collectors of Jesus's time. The tax collectors were hated because they were Jews who turned against their own people to collect taxes for the Romans; often they also took more money than was necessary to line their own pockets. Nobody liked them. Some of our students can be like that, too. They don't fit in with others, and they "tax" our patience because of the extra time and attention they require.

Let's look at three saints who handled challenging students and ask for their intercession.

Love the Unruly Child: St. John Bosco

John (Don) Bosco (1815–1888), the patron saint of schoolchildren, started schools for the poor in Italy. He adopted a style of disciplining unruly students that was revolutionary for his time.

John Bosco grew up near the foot of the Italian Alps. His dad, a peasant farmer, died when he was two, leaving his mom to raise John and his two brothers. A fun-loving boy, John played tricks on his friends and learned to juggle and do acrobatic acts.

John knew early in life that he would serve children. At age nine, he had a dream in which he was put in charge of a group of boys who swore and were generally very undisciplined. In this dream, the Virgin Mary appeared to him and explained, "This is your field . . . it's where you must labor."[1] The boys in his dream appeared as wild animals and then turned into lambs. Throughout his life, Don Bosco (as he was later called) continued to have dreams that guided his decisions and helped him find his purpose in educating the poor.

The fulfillment of that childhood dream came about in 1846, when John was sent to work as a priest in Turin. At the time, Turin had become industrialized so quickly that the population had tripled. People had flocked to the town looking for work. Sadly, there were far more job seekers than there were jobs, so many ended up unemployed and living in slums.

John began working with other priests in prison ministry. It was not unusual for twelve- and thirteen-year-olds to be sentenced to prison, which usually led to a lifelong cycle of incarcerations. These boys reminded John of his childhood dream, and he believed this cycle of imprisonment could be broken if someone showed authentic concern.

Obviously, these boys were not model schoolchildren. In fact, they often didn't go to school at all. And so, the good priest began to connect with them where they were. According to one story, when a sexton at John's church reprimanded a boy who had entered the church to get warm, John spoke to the boy gently, taught him some prayers, and told him to come back on Sunday with friends. The boy did just that, bringing four poor friends with him.

How did John get these boys to keep returning for lessons and prayer? He relied on skills he had mastered as a child. He started holding what he called "oratories," in which he used his juggling, magic tricks, and acrobatic skills to entertain them. However, the boys had to take part in prayers and lessons first. The group grew until there were three hundred street boys at these oratories! They were too loud to gather near the orphanage where Bosco worked as a chaplain, so he moved the group to a nearby field.

Finally, John bought a home and then expanded it so that he could take in boarders. His mother came to help him care for the boys. He fed and clothed them, helped them find jobs, instructed them in the faith, and taught them to read and write. Within a few years, he was caring for 500 boys, including 150 boarders.

Though many were thought to be juvenile delinquents, thieves, and gamblers, John knew how to get their attention. Once, he saw a group of boys gambling in the street in Turin. He asked to join their game. He ended up winning all their money but promised to give it back if they came to Mass on Sunday. The boys did just that.

To keep the students excited and engaged, John continued to mix learning with play. After praying the Rosary, singing hymns, or listening to a sermon, the students were treated to tricks and acrobatics from John. He took his students on field trips and wrote a play to teach them the metric system. His motto was, "Enjoy yourself as much as you like—if only you keep from sin."[2]

Even though John was teaching the unruliest boys of Turin, he did not deliver harsh punishments. He believed people learned best when encouraged. Thus, when a boy misbehaved, he would often offer a *parola all'orecchio* ("word in the ear"). Instead of reprimanding the boy loudly and publicly, he would whisper a word of advice or encouragement to the boy.

By 1869, Don Bosco founded the Salesian order, a group of religious brothers who opened schools employing his unique methods. He wanted the environment within his schools to mimic that of family life because he believed students would follow instruction and guidance if their teachers had first won their confidence and admiration.

WHAT CAN WE LEARN FROM ST. JOHN BOSCO?

John Bosco didn't have success with every challenging student. When a student didn't respond to his *parola all'orecchio*, he followed a set of guidelines for escalating the consequences: warning them repeatedly (but privately), giving indirect advice (by talking up the opposite virtue of the student's vice), and using others (teachers and classmates) to influence the student. He warned his teachers never to dole out punishment in a moment of anger, but to take time to pray and calm down first. When his other methods failed, John would withhold outward signs of fatherly affection. His boys admired John so much that they did not want to be left out. If even these harsher consequences didn't work, he occasionally resorted to expelling students from his school.

John's approach to training both students and future teachers was not foolproof—a few of the boys he tried to prepare for priesthood ended up leaving. Yet he still gives us food for thought about how we approach our students.

- *Redirect behavior in a way that respects the dignity of the child.* St. John Bosco's example reminds me of some former coworkers who were known for pulling students out into the hallway for private chats (instead of "yelling" at the students in front of everyone). St. John's words and my coworkers' examples remind me that I should employ this technique more often myself. How can I offer a *parola all'orecchio* the next time a student needs redirection?
- *Mix in the fun with the serious.* At one point, everyone in education talked about "time on task" from "bell to bell." While I certainly don't want to waste time, there are educational benefits to throwing in some fun now and then. Kids need brain breaks. Plenty of scientific research has shown that students perform better on standardized tests if they are given a break between sections. I might not be able to juggle and perform acrobatic tricks for my students, but I can add in a little choice activity time or a short extra recess if students stay focused and finish their work in class.
- *Don't be afraid of a little noise.* St. John Bosco reminds us that kids are kids, and sometimes things are going to get a little loud. Early in my career, I thought my classroom always had to be perfectly quiet. Collaborative projects made me nervous—so much noise in the room! However, St. John Bosco's approach was to "shout, sing, dance, if you want. The important thing is that you do not offend God. Nevertheless, don't damage my walls too much!"[3]

Calm Stressed-Out Students: St. Dorotheus of Gaza

Born in the early part of the sixth century, Dorotheus received a classical education, but he yearned for a secluded life. Eventually, he founded his own monastery, where he took charge of other young monks. This is where he met a challenging student named Dositheus, whose behavior vacillated wildly from acting out one day to zealously overcorrecting himself the next.

As Dorotheus got to know the wealthy young man, he discovered the reason for his behavior. On a trip to Jerusalem, Dositheus had seen a painting of tormented souls in hell. Anxious that he would meet the same fate, the young man asked a nearby woman what to do to avoid hell. She told him to pray and fast. Dositheus took this advice to heart and soon joined the monastery where Dorotheus resided.

As this young man's mentor, Dorotheus had to find a way to temper Dositheus's wild behavioral swings. Dorotheus helped him to change gradually. When Dositheus ate six pounds of bread a day, Dorotheus urged him to curb such gluttony by eating a little less each day until he reached a moderate amount (rather than resort to extreme fasting).

Dositheus was also known to have a terrible temper. Although he learned to control it, he still struggled at times. Once when he lost control of himself, he ran back to his cell and fell on the floor, inconsolable from the terrible guilt. Doretheus reminded him that Christ still loved him and he need not beat himself up over his lapses.

Toward the end of his life, Dositheus became ill and could no longer do the hospital work he had enjoyed so much. He could not even fast as he used to do. Dorotheus reassured him that it was okay to spend his final days focused on prayer. That and his desire to be with Christ were enough. Both Dorotheus and his protégé Dositheus were canonized.

WHAT CAN WE LEARN FROM ST. DOROTHEUS OF GAZA?

When I read about Dositheus's erratic behavior, I think of some of my students who seem not to care about their grades one day and then get visibly upset when they receive an A instead of an A+ on a particular assignment. They fear they won't get into a good college unless they get straight A+s. When I point out that they can still be admitted to a good college even if they get the occasional B, they look at me like I'm crazy—"But my parents are going to kill me!"

Their reaction reminds me of Dositheus, who thought God wouldn't love him if he gave in to temptation now and then. For some students, their future happiness and self-worth seem to depend on achieving straight As. Sadly, this attitude creates an incredible amount of stress and anxiety—feelings that are often reinforced by parental expectations. So how are we as educators to deal with this perfectionist attitude?

- *Respond with compassion.* Reassure your students that their worth is not dependent on their grades. Share stories of students and family members who did not excel in high school but who blossomed in college and went on to become very successful adults.
- *Help your students discover their identity as a child of God.* The dignity of every human being is found not in what they've done but in the fact that they are children of God. St. Dorotheus knew this was true about his charge, St. Dositheus, and now they are both in the Communion of Saints!

Encourage Reluctant Students: St. Jean-Baptiste de La Salle

Nearly two hundred years before Don Bosco was taking in poor juvenile delinquents in Italy, Jean-Baptiste de La Salle (1651–1719) was tending to a similar clientele in France. His first students were boys, ages ten to fourteen, known to be "wild."[4] They gambled, committed petty crimes, and fought. Yet even the most reluctant scholars eventually greeted Jean-Baptiste and his fellow teachers with joy each morning. How did it happen?

In seventeenth-century France, education was mostly for wealthy boys, who were generally tutored privately in their homes. Other

higher-class boys might attend grammar schools attached to universities, where Latin was the primary language of instruction. Some
charity schools (attached to parishes) did exist. However, boys from
poor families often could not afford the supplies—or they needed to
work to earn an income for their family. In addition, the education
provided by charity schools was deemed impractical by poor families.
Why would a future laborer need to read Latin? And why was writing
taught only at designated "writing schools" that the poor could not
afford?

Jean-Baptiste took a completely different approach. His teachers
instructed the boys in their native French (because being able to communicate properly in their native tongue would be much more useful
to them), and they included both reading and writing instruction,
for Jean-Baptiste believed that "the child that knows how to read and
write will be capable of anything."[5] In addition, his schools had a vocational focus; he knew that poor parents would not send their children
to school unless they thought they would learn something useful.

Even more radical than his ideas on what to teach these "wild"
boys were Jean-Baptiste's beliefs on how they should be treated. When
Jean-Baptiste took over the charity schools, he invited the poorly educated schoolmasters to stay at his large family home so that he could
better train them. Many of his family members found this intolerable,
so one relative (who had a claim to the family home) sued him and
ended up winning. Jean-Baptiste then had to find a new home for
himself and his teachers.

Jean-Baptiste de La Salle trained his teachers to see their students
in a new way: "Recognize Jesus beneath the poor rags of the children
whom you have to instruct. Adore him in them."[6] He didn't want his
educators to think of their students as members of the lower class. He
encouraged them to view the students as being among the wealthi-
est children on earth because they were made in the image of God.
Similar to John Bosco's approach to creating a family atmosphere,
Jean-Baptiste de La Salle wanted the students to know their human
dignity and worth as children of God.

When it came to management and discipline in his schools, Jean-Baptiste wrote a pedagogical text titled *The Conduct of the Christian Schools*. Here he explained his beliefs on managing student misbehavior. Punishment, he insisted, should not outweigh the crime. When confronting misbehavior, a teacher should not immediately reject the student's excuse. When a student gets too loud, the teacher should lower their voice to get them to listen. Isn't that the opposite of the approach we might be inclined to use?

WHAT CAN WE LEARN FROM ST. JEAN-BAPTISTE DE LA SALLE?

As the patron saint of teachers of youth, St. Jean-Baptiste de La Salle has a lot of advice to offer.

- *Remember that students are more likely to cooperate if they feel respected.* Jean-Baptiste was adamant that teachers and students show each other mutual respect. He reminded teachers that they are God's ambassadors to their students. Do I take that to heart when I'm in the classroom? While my head knows that each student is worthy of love and respect as one of God's children, it can be really hard to recognize Jesus in them when their behavior seems less than Christlike. But just as Mother Teresa saw the face of Christ in all the poor she served, so must we try our best to remember that we are serving Christ when we serve our students.
- *Avoid snap judgments and harsh responses.* St. Jean-Baptiste de La Salle's words about not immediately rejecting students' excuses remind me to slow down and not be quick to judge. When I started teaching, if I saw a student lean toward a classmate in the middle of a test as if about to speak, I would yell out, "No talking!" Later I learned to ask, "Do you need something?" Sometimes the student simply broke a pencil tip and needed a sharpener. In those cases, I was happy to help out, and I avoided embarrassing the child who was just trying to finish her test. Other times, of course, the student was about to cheat, and I would get a quick "no thank you" in response. Handling the situation in this way

accomplished several things: (1) the student knew I was watching her, (2) we avoided the punishment that would have come if actual cheating had occurred, and (3) the student was redirected in a way that didn't compromise her dignity.

• *"Teach to the test?"* Jean-Baptiste made his schools' curriculum as practical and useful as possible in order to engage both students and parents. Many teachers today feel the pressure to "teach to the test" in order to raise their students' scores. But St. Jean-Baptiste de La Salle reminds us that this approach will not interest many of our students. To get our reluctant learners to buy into our lessons, we need to look at whether or not our lessons seem useful to them.

For example, can you adapt assignments so they have real-world applications? Instead of lengthy research reports that only the teacher reads, have the students create "video essays" (think documentary-style films with voice-over narrations) that can be shared with the whole class. Many older students already have their own YouTube channels, so making a video will seem more "real world" to them than a ten-page essay.

Saint Squad Summary: Show Curiosity, Not Judgment

One August, I sat in yet another back-to-school in-service day, doing my best to muster up enthusiasm, although the previous school year had completely drained me. One of the administrators showed a short clip from the TV show *Ted Lasso*, in which Ted talks about seeing a quote often attributed to Walt Whitman painted on a wall: "Be curious, not judgmental."

That quote is the key to how the saints in this chapter handled bright yet challenging students. When students presented these teachers with behaviors such as gambling, noisy outbursts, anxiety and perfectionism, lack of enthusiasm, or even stealing, the teachers took the time to be curious about *why* they acted this way. They got to know the students and their needs, and then they went after the root of the problem.

So the next time you're faced with a student whose behavior challenges your usual classroom-management techniques, try being curious. Ask yourself questions like these:

- Is the child who's snacking in the middle of class not eating breakfast before school? Is he going through a growth spurt? Is his blood sugar low?
- Why won't that child stop annoying her classmates? Does she not get enough attention at home? Is she getting bullied and trying to create a safe space for herself? Does she struggle to make friends?
- Why does that child constantly ask to visit the bathroom? Is he cutting class for a little social time or mischief, or does he have a medical condition? Does he have undiagnosed ADHD? Is he anxious and just needs a moment out of the spotlight?
- Why does that child wear long sleeves during warm weather? Is she hiding bruises inflicted by family members or cuts she made on her own arms? Or is it simply her favorite shirt, and she uses it as a security blanket?

Be curious, not judgmental. It's so tempting to jump to conclusions about our students—to assume we know exactly why they are acting out. However, if we take time to be curious and truly get to know our students, we will not only win their trust and respect but will meet some fascinating individuals.

REFLECTION QUESTIONS

1. St. John Bosco used a *parola all'orecchio* (word in the ear) to redirect students. What would you do next if those quiet words don't have the intended effect?
2. St. Dorotheus consoled and guided St. Dositheus. How have you guided students who go to extremes and lose faith in themselves?
3. St. Jean-Baptiste de La Salle recognized students' dignity and worth. How have you done the same in your classroom?

FOUR

Saints Who Advocated for Change

Teaching is the work most suited to draw down the graces of God if it is done with purity of intention, without distinction between the poor and the rich, between relatives and friends and strangers, between the pretty and the ugly, the gentle and the grumblers, looking upon them all as drops of Our Lord's blood.
—St. Marguerite Bourgeoys

We know that many Catholic schools were started by congregations of priests or religious brothers or sisters, but that doesn't mean they all started out perfectly. Many saints fought for change in their schools and institutions so that they could better serve God's people. When we see injustices in our schools, or simply better practices to employ, here is a little squad of saints we can implore to give us strength, patience, and wisdom as we work for change.

Be Humble When Promoting Change: Bl. Marie-Anne Blondin

Bl. Marie-Anne Blondin (1809–1890) is known as the patron of the education of the poor. She was born Esther Blondin to a poor farming family in Quebec, Canada. Her devout parents taught her to love the Eucharist, be patient in suffering, and trust in God. Like many poor French-Canadian families at that time, her parents were both illiterate, and as a child she did not have any formal schooling.

At age twenty-two, Esther became a housemaid for the Congregation of Notre Dame and enrolled in their school to learn to read and write. She tried to enter the convent but left due to poor health. Determined to help others rise out of poverty, she began teaching at a parochial school for girls in Vaudreuil. At the time, boys and girls were educated separately, and Church rules required boys to be taught only by men and girls to be taught only by women. Since many parishes could not afford two schools, they had either one or none. In 1848, Esther asked Bishop Ignace Bourget if she could start a religious congregation that would teach boys and girls together so that more poor children could receive an education.

On September 8, 1850, Esther founded the Congregation of the Sisters of St. Anne and became its superior under the name Mother Marie-Anne. In 1853, Bishop Bourget moved the motherhouse of this rapidly growing community to St. Jacques de l'Achigan, where Fr. Louis-Adolphe Maréchal became its chaplain. Unfortunately, Fr. Maréchal's decisions proved to be more disruptive than supportive. For example, while Mother Marie-Anne was away, he increased the students' boarding fees. He also told the sisters to go to Confession only when he was available. In 1854, Fr. Maréchal asked Bishop Bourget to remove Mother Marie-Anne from her position, and she ended up doing laundry and other routine tasks for the order she had begun.

To encourage her sisters, Mother Marie-Anne told them, "May the Holy Eucharist and perfect abandonment to God's will be your heaven on earth."[1] Her humility and obedience in the face of injustice not only ensured the continuation of her community but also inspired the young novices. When asked by one of them why she was willing to do such humble tasks despite being their foundress, she replied, "The deeper a tree sinks its roots into the soil, the greater are its chances of growing and producing fruit."[2]

WHAT CAN WE LEARN FROM BL. MARIE-ANNE BLONDIN?

Although Bl. Marie-Anne Blondin was treated terribly by her chaplain, she made good changes in the educational system. Thanks to her, more poor children received an education in classrooms where boys and girls could learn together.

- *Humility can bear great fruit.* The humiliation of the foundress's demotion turned out to be a great gift to the order. Removed from her administrative role, Marie-Anne was able to spend more time with the novices, preparing them for their work as educators. As a result, her congregation continued to grow and expand. Imagine if Marie-Anne had given in to despair or fought the chaplain. He might have called for the disbanding of her congregation altogether. Instead of risking the future of her order, she focused on her primary goal: the education of the children. To her, that was far more important than her own ego.
- *Set an example of humility for others.* Not only did Bl. Marie-Anne's humility ensure the survival of her order, but it also provided her novices with a good example of how to serve with a humble heart. I can be tempted to gripe about things at school, but if I complain in front of my students, what kind of example am I setting?

Move from Discussion to Action: St. John of Ávila

The patron of both priests and educators, John of Ávila (1499–1569) was born near Toledo, Spain. While studying law at the University of Salamanca, he had such a strong conversion experience that he left school and spent a few years in solitude to discern his vocation. He studied for the priesthood and was ordained in 1526.

Originally, John wanted to be a missionary priest to North America. However, after hearing his preaching, the archbishop of Seville persuaded him to stay in Spain. When he preached, thousands flocked to hear him. Afterward, many reformed their ways and sought holiness. Evidence of this exists in John's correspondence with his converts. He was also known as an excellent spiritual director and teacher. When asked by a young priest how to become a good preacher, John simply told him to love God above all.

In order to bring about the reform necessary for the Church, John insisted that it was time to move from discussion to action. Already, the bishops had shared plenty of opinions about how the Church should be reformed. John told them it was time to "excuse ourselves from deliberation and take up the task of putting into practice something that fell into disuse because of the sins and calamities of the Church."[3] Specifically, he wanted the bishops to begin by examining their own lives. Were they living as true representatives of Christ? Were they acting as servants to the priests under their care or like masters dealing with slaves?

When it came to reforming the priesthood, John focused on two areas. First, he emphasized rigorous, high standards for accepting men into the seminary. Too many men with worldly ambitions wanted to become priests for the wrong reasons. John suggested making entrance into seminaries so difficult that those unfit for the priesthood would be discouraged from applying.

Second, he believed that candidates for the priesthood needed intense programs of study. Recognizing that proper education is essential to vocations, he founded schools for children and adults, including colleges that led to the seminary system as we know it today. John believed that men studying for the priesthood needed to live in a communal setting, just as he had lived in a loosely defined community of priests in his early years. They also needed a thorough understanding of scripture and doctrine. This would seem obvious to us nowadays, but at the time, John found that many clergy had not been properly trained in the Church's teachings.

John was friends with other Spanish saints who were concerned with reform and education, including St. Teresa of Ávila (who reformed the Carmelite order) and St. Ignatius of Loyola (who founded the Jesuits). Imagine having saint friends like those as part of your professional learning community!

WHAT CAN WE LEARN FROM ST. JOHN OF ÁVILA?

When I first read about St. John of Ávila reforming the training of priests, I didn't think much of it because I had not realized how lax the requirements for becoming a priest were at the time. It's rather shocking to think there were priests who didn't have a strong grasp on Christian doctrine. Then again, I'm sure we've all run into educators who do not have as strong a grasp on a subject matter as we expect.

- *Invest in the next generation of educators.* St. John of Ávila saw the importance of preparing the next generation of priests, and it's a good thing he did. Our seminaries need to prepare priests for the challenges of their vocation, just as our universities need to prepare teachers for the challenges they will face. Some universities are changing the way education majors proceed through their clinical hours by introducing them to classroom teaching before their actual student teaching. When I was an undergrad, student teaching was left to the last semester, and even though we clocked more than one hundred clinical hours, many were still overwhelmed by student teaching and decided to switch careers before they had even donned their graduation gown. Let's ask St. John of Ávila to pray for us and those preparing the next generation of teachers. We need professionals who are not only experts in their content areas but also prepared to handle the countless challenges that often drive educators out of the field early on.

- *Look in the mirror before you insist on someone else's reform.* John told the bishops to reform themselves before asking their priests to change. This approach can be applied to our school systems as well. Do administrators look to improve themselves before asking their teachers to do the same? Do teachers look to improve themselves before asking their students to have a growth mindset?

Seek Wise Counsel: St. Charles Borromeo

Charles Borromeo (1538–1584) became the patron saint of catechists and seminarians despite the fact that he was initially believed to be unintelligent because of a childhood speech impediment. Despite his verbal limitations, Charles loved to study and earned a doctorate in civil and canon law by the age of twenty-one. That same year, his uncle (Pope Pius IV) made him a cardinal-deacon and the administrator of the Milan diocese. He helped his uncle reconvene the Council of Trent and drafted the council's catechism. He went on to found seminaries that became examples for other dioceses.

Charles also set about reforming his own diocese in Milan, and he wasn't afraid to change things up in order to get the work done. When one group of cathedral canons refused to cooperate with him on reforms, he created a new order of priests to work with him.

Furthermore, Charles made a point of visiting each parish in the diocese personally to address any areas that needed reform. For example, he had been told of an old priest who had fallen into sinful patterns of behavior that scandalized the community. Charles sent for the priest and spoke with him privately. At first, the people of the town were upset that there was no public rebuke of the priest. However, they soon found that the man had made a complete change in his behavior after one brief meeting with the cardinal. This is not to suggest that the priest's bad behavior was swept under a rug. Rather, it's a reminder that getting to the root of a problem does not have to involve public humiliation.

WHAT CAN WE LEARN FROM ST. CHARLES BORROMEO?

The story of St. Charles Borromeo and his speech impediment reminds me of Moses, who is believed to have spoken with a stutter. With support from the right friends, firm determination, and faith in God, both men successfully changed the sinful ways of those around them. How can you do the same?

- *Find your support group.* When Charles set out to reform the Milan diocese, the group of priests who were supposed to support him refused, so he found other priests to help him. I'm grateful to have several circles of educator friends I can rely on. Some are at my current school, and others are from previous schools, graduate courses, online connections, and church. St. Charles reminds me that when I don't receive the support I need from one group, it doesn't mean I can't find it elsewhere. If our ideas for reform are in the students' best interests, we can find like-minded educators out there to help.
- *Remember that reform requires both firm determination and gentleness.* Getting people to change their ways isn't easy. We've all had experiences trying to bring about a change in our programs that has not gone exactly as we had hoped. During my teenage years, my mom worked as the director of religious education at our parish. Occasionally, she would share stories about her lay catechists. While many were great, a few weren't on the same page as everyone else. One still wanted to use the *Baltimore Catechism*;

another decided to "wait until the students were ready" to begin his lessons, so kids often socialized for most of the period.

The way biographers have described Charles reminds me of my mom. They were both determined in their actions but gentle in their approach. My mom had tough conversations with some of her catechists, and once or twice, she had to "un-volunteer" a few of them. But changes won't happen unless we resolve to make them happen. Let us pray that when we must have difficult conversations about needed reforms, St. Charles Borromeo will remind us to take action with gentleness and a firm resolve.

Trust God for the Outcome: St. Marguerite Bourgeoys

Marguerite Bourgeoys (1620–1700) began her teaching career by educating poor children in Troyes, France, as an extern sister of the Congregation of Troyes. In 1653, the governor of the Ville-Marie settlement in Canada invited her to come and teach. A few years later, she converted a stone stable into her first school. She focused on educating girls because she believed that family was the key to building a strong community. With the help of several other women, including two Iroquois, she opened day schools and more boarding schools. In 1676, this group of women became the Congregation of Notre Dame.

Marguerite wanted her order to be out in the community rather than cloistered. Msgr. François de Laval, the first bishop of Quebec, disagreed. For a while, the nuns lived in a convent, but a fire destroyed it in 1683. The bishop continued to oppose the sisters not being cloistered, but in 1698 his successor finally relented. At that point, Marguerite had already relinquished her role as superior, and the congregation had more than two hundred schools.

WHAT CAN WE LEARN FROM ST. MARGUERITE BOURGEOYS?

The sixth of twelve children, Marguerite grew up in a comfortable, middle-class Christian home in France, but she was not afraid to leave it all behind to follow her calling on the other side of the world. Despite the challenges she faced in her new environment, she made the best of her situation and held on to the hope that a thriving community would emerge.

- *Strong families make for strong communities.* While many at the time saw the education of girls as frivolous since most girls would marry and raise children, Marguerite believed that a good education for girls meant stronger families, which would in turn create stronger communities. How has your school worked to strengthen families for the sake of the larger community?
- *Sometimes the reform we seek will occur after we're gone.* Marguerite had retired from her role as the congregation's superior when permission was finally granted for her sisters to live outside the cloister. I'm sure she was happy to have her sisters out in the community, but at the same time, I wouldn't blame her if she felt frustration at how long it took for this request to be granted. And really all it took was a new bishop being appointed. How many times has this happened in our schools? You've got a great idea, but there's that one person (administrator, pastor, school board member) who seems to be standing in the way, and nothing can be done until that person steps down.

    I don't know why this happens. Perhaps God is teaching us patience, but St. Marguerite Bourgeoys's story gives us reason to hope. Maybe we won't see the change we want right away, but that doesn't mean it's not worth fighting for or that we should give up faith that it will come one day.

Saint Squad Summary: Get Used to Different

If you follow me on any social media, you know I'm a huge fan of the TV show *The Chosen*, the first multi-season show about Christ and his followers. In the episode where Jesus calls Matthew to follow him, Simon protests because Matthew is a tax collector, and Jesus tells him, "Get used to different."

That tagline works well for the show as a whole. *The Chosen* not only tells the gospels in long form with plenty of backstory to fill in the details the evangelists didn't include but also summarizes Jesus's whole ministry. The ancient Jews were expecting the Messiah to be a revolutionary who would overthrow the Romans. Jesus was revolutionary, just not the military kind the Jews expected. This brought Jesus into conflict with a lot of people, such as the Zealots, who were training for war, and many of the Pharisees who believed Jesus was blaspheming. There was no way someone like *him* could possibly be the Messiah.

When we're trying to revolutionize the way things are done in schools, some people might view us as they viewed Jesus, as someone with crazy ideas at best or as dangerous at worst. Just as Jesus's ideas didn't win everyone over at first, so our ideas might take a while to catch on. Of course, we should have humility. Perhaps what we thought would be great isn't the best idea after all. Or maybe an idea is not taking hold right away because it needs to germinate some more. Then again perhaps it's a fabulous idea, and it will just take time for others to grasp how good it is. In the meantime, let's ask Bl. Marie-Anne Blondin, St. John of Ávila, St. Charles Borromeo, and St. Marguerite Bourgeoys to pray for us and our desires for reform. If they are worthy of merit, may God grant us the wisdom and the patience to see them to fruition.

REFLECTION QUESTIONS

1. Bl. Marie-Anne Blondin served humbly. When has God asked you to humble yourself in order to bring about change?
2. St. John of Ávila told bishops to examine themselves before requiring reform from others. What changes might you need to make before asking others to do the same?
3. St. Charles Borromeo acted firmly but gently when helping others to reform. How can you find the right balance between being firm and being gentle?
4. St. Marguerite Bourgeoys trusted God to help her bring about change in her new community despite the challenges. When has your trust in God paid off?

FIVE

Saints Who Sought Justice for Their Students

Peacefully do at each moment what at the moment needs to be done.

—St. Katharine Drexel

The 1954 Supreme Court case *Brown v. Board of Education of Topeka* sought to undo some of the injustices in education brought about by the "separate but equal" policies of the Jim Crow era. Those of us in education know that injustices in education continue to exist to this day with regard to funding, hiring practices, accessibility, and inclusion.

Long before *Brown v. Board of Education*, saints around the world fought against injustices toward their pupils. They strove to create a learning environment where students were free from abuse, treated with dignity, and educated with compassion regardless of their age, ethnicity, culture, or socioeconomic level.

Protect God's Children: St. Charles Lwanga and Companions

I was teaching at my second Catholic school when the Archdiocese of Chicago adopted the VIRTUS training program in response to the wave of sexual abuse scandals that had just come to light. If I had known about St. Charles Lwanga (1860–1886) at the time, I would have asked for his intercession. Not only did he protect young boys from a pedophilic king, but he gave his life to do so.

To understand how St. Charles Lwanga and his companions became martyrs who stood up for chastity and against sexual abuse, it helps to know a bit of history. In the 1880s, Protestant and Catholic missionaries went to Buganda, a kingdom in Uganda, and after a short time were sent out of the country. Three years later, they were invited back by King Mwanga, who had been persuaded by his majordomo, Joseph Mukasa, a leading catechist in the Christian community.

Joseph was in charge of approximately four hundred boys who had been selected to serve the king as pages. Some of the boys were baptized Christians or studying for baptism. Tragically, the king was a pedophile, and when the boys learned that the king's demands were sinful, they refused his sexual advances and appealed to Joseph for help. To protect the boys, Joseph hid them in his own house or sent them away on errands. Witch doctors and chiefs eventually convinced the young king, who suffered from alcoholism and mental instability in addition to his sexual obsessions, that these Christians would undermine his power.

When Joseph criticized the king for his debauchery and for killing a Protestant missionary, King Mwanga had Joseph beheaded and vowed to rid his country of Christianity. Charles Lwanga then took over as majordomo of the pages. Like Joseph, Charles continued to catechize the boys, baptized several, and tried to protect them from the king.

In May 1886, the king returned from a hunt to find all the Christian pages missing. When the first page returned, he confessed that sixteen-year-old Denis Ssebuggwawo had been teaching him a religion lesson. The king found Denis and threw a spear through the young catechist's neck. Then King Mwanga told all the pages to renounce their faith immediately or face death. None of the Christian pages were willing to deny their faith.

On June 3, 1886, Charles Lwanga, his fellow catechists, and the pages (ages thirteen to twenty-five) were marched to Namugongo. Charles was martyred first. His legs were held over a flaming pyre so that they burned first. Charles prayed quietly until the end, his final words being, "My God!" The rest of the young men were then burned together. In all, thirteen Catholics, eleven Protestants, and eight more boys who had yet to be baptized were martyred that day. To the astonishment of the executioners, none of the boys whined or complained. All of them murmured quiet prayers until the end.

WHAT CAN WE LEARN FROM ST. CHARLES LWANGA AND HIS COMPANIONS?

This was the hardest reflection for me to write because I am sickened by the sexual abuses that have plagued not only our Church but the entire world. Thank God for brave people like Charles and Joseph who stand up against pedophiles. Praise God for those men and women in our own day who have bravely come forward to share their stories or to report cases.

- *Pray for courage to stand up for the abused.* If you are teaching or volunteering at a Catholic school or parish, you've been trained to look for the warning signs, so there's nothing new that I can tell you. I only offer you this thought: If you do suspect a case of sexual abuse in your school or religious education program or anywhere, pray for the intercession of St. Joseph Mukasa and St. Charles Lwanga so that the Holy Spirit gives you the courage and the wisdom to do what is right.

- *Pray for courage to talk openly about God's call to chastity.* It took a lot of courage for Joseph and Charles to explain to the young boys that the king's demands were sinful. These couldn't have been easy conversations. As someone who taught junior high religion (which included some basic theology of the body lessons), I know how difficult (and countercultural!) these discussions can be with young people. I've also heard from some millennial friends how the "purity culture" they were raised in made them "irrationally ashamed of everything associated with the body."[1] May St. Charles Lwanga and his companions intercede for us so that our students will know what a gift from God our bodies are.

Create Opportunities: St. Katharine Drexel and Servant of God Nicholas Black Elk

Katharine Drexel (1856–1955) was born to a wealthy Philadelphia banker and his wife, who died only a few weeks after her daughter's birth. Her dad went on to marry Emma Bouvier, who proved to be a loving and influential stepmom to "Kate" (as her family called her) and her older sister, Elizabeth.

The new Mrs. Drexel believed that God had given their family money to help others. She often brought her two stepdaughters and her own daughter, Louise, with her when she distributed food, medicine, clothing, and rent money to those in need. She taught the three young girls not only to be generous but also to recognize the dignity of the people they served. After both parents died, the three young women inherited an estate worth $14 million.

Well-educated and well-traveled, Katharine saw firsthand the devastating effects that poverty, racism, and discrimination had on Native Americans and Black Americans. Wanting to help, Katharine traveled to Rome to ask Pope Leo XIII to send priests to serve in the missions. When he suggested she become a missionary herself, her first reaction was to cry and become physically ill. Accepting God's call is not always easy! If you've read *Sweet Jesus, Is It June Yet?*, you already know about my own call to teach; I cried just like St. Katharine and spent many mornings during my first year of teaching feeling nauseated.

However, after returning to America and consulting with Archbishop Patrick Ryan and her friend Bishop James O'Connor, Katharine decided to start her own order of religious sisters to care for Native Americans and Black Americans. Specifically, she saw education as a way to lift them out of poverty. Thus, she founded the Sisters of the Blessed Sacrament in 1891, using her inheritance to open about sixty schools for Indigenous and Black Americans.

In 1915, the Sisters of the Blessed Sacrament opened Xavier Preparatory High School in New Orleans. Two years later, they opened a school for training Black educators. In 1925, they opened Xavier University of Louisiana, America's only historically Black and Catholic university. At its opening, the university consisted of a College of Liberal Arts and Sciences; another college was added two years later. Dr. Sharlene Sinegal-DeCuir, an associate professor of history at Xavier, provides insight into Katharine's awareness of racial prejudice. Speaking of the university's opening, Dr. Sinegal-DeCuir explains, "During the dedication of the building, Katharine Drexel knew black people could not sit unless all white men were seated first so she did away with all the chairs so that everyone was equal when they came to Xavier. White men stood. Black men stood."[2]

Despite her vast fortune, Katharine chose to live a simple lifestyle. She traveled third class, used scraps of paper for her notes, and even refused hospitality from relatives if she feared setting a bad example for her fellow sisters. As an educator, she thought she was too gentle on her students but took care to make sure her schools were staffed with competent teachers. Because so much of her spiritual writing, business records, letters, and travel reports have been archived by the Sisters of the Blessed Sacrament, we can infer that she was witty, had good business sense, and could be very strict about following rules, but was also very much loved.

One of the locations that Katharine funded later became the main building at the Red Cloud Indian Mission on the Pine Ridge Reservation, which included Holy Rosary Church. As I was researching St. Katharine Drexel, news broke of ground-penetrating radars finding what appeared to be mass unmarked graves at schools for Native Americans in Canada and the United States. My research to learn more about the treatment of Indigenous people at residential schools led me to a Native American man who worked at Holy Rosary Church and whose cause for canonization has been opened in recent years. His name is Nicholas Black Elk.

Although no official birth record exists, Nicholas Black Elk (1858–1950), commonly known as Black Elk, was born in the region now known as South Dakota to an Oglala Lakota family. As a child, he had a mystical dream in which he saw all of the Creator's children being united under the protection of a large tree. As an adult, he had another mystical vision after a Ghost Dance, in which he saw the same tree, but this time a man (of an origin Black Elk didn't recognize) stood in front of the tree with wounds in his hands. When combined, Black Elk saw these two visions as being a call to his vocation, even though he didn't fully understand immediately.

Before becoming Catholic, Black Elk became a skilled warrior. As a child, he was present at the Wounded Knee Massacre. When he was twelve, he participated in the Battle of the Little Bighorn. In 1890, he fought in the aftermath of the Wounded Knee Massacre. He also spent two years touring Europe with Buffalo Bill Cody.

At this time, the US government allowed all reservations to have only one religious denomination, and the Pine Ridge Reservation, where Black Elk lived, was designated as Episcopalian. However, Chief Red Cloud petitioned for the "Black Robes" (Jesuit priests) to come to his people. He saw in the Jesuits a chance to retain some of their Native culture. All schools (public and private) were required to follow certain government policies. Lessons could be taught only in English. Students were forbidden to communicate in other languages and had to cut their long hair and wear Western clothes in school. While the Jesuits enforced these policies (a decision they later apologized for), they did see connections between Native American spirituality and Catholicism that opened a doorway to conversion.

When a Jesuit protested against Black Elk's work as a medicine man on a sick boy who had been baptized, the two of them argued. However, within a week, Black Elk was seeking out the same priest for instruction in the Christian faith. In 1904, he was baptized on St. Nicholas's feast day and received his new first name. In 1905, he married a Catholic widow with two children, and in 1907 they had a daughter together.

By that time, Black Elk had already learned so much about the faith and proved himself to be such a natural preacher that he was asked to become a catechist. He spent nearly fifty years as a Catholic and more than forty years as a catechist. Some of his former students are still alive and describe him as kind and gentle—a man who truly led a holy life. He continued to hold on to many of his Lakota traditions while preaching the Catholic faith. Those who knew him said he was as comfortable holding a prayer pipe as he was praying the Rosary as he walked to Mass. At a time when many Native Americans were being stripped of their culture, their language, and their beliefs, Nicholas Black Elk found a way to stay true to his culture's traditions and to the Catholic faith.

A note about the mass graves: At the time this book is going to print, news has broken that no human remains were found at an Indian boarding school in Manitoba, where ground-penetrating radar had originally identified what appeared to be mass graves.[3] Further research led me to the website for Truth and Healing at the Holy Rosary Mission where Black Elk lived and catechized. The goal of Truth and Healing is to acknowledge and examine the trauma that is part of their history as an Indian boarding school. Ground-penetrating radar used at Holy Rosary Mission originally suggested a few possible sites of unmarked graves; however, excavations at those sites discovered no human remains.[4]

Obviously, there is far more to be discovered and discussed than I can offer in this short section, and new information will come to light in coming days and years. If you are interested in learning more, I recommend visiting the school's website (https://www.redcloudschool. org/) and listening to Episode 213 of the *Catholic School Matters* podcast, in which Dr. Timothy Uhl talks with Maka Black Elk, a direct descendent of Nicholas Black Elk, who was the Executive Director of Truth and Healing at the time of the interview.

Let's us pray for healing and reconciliation. May the intercessions of St. Katharine Drexel, who desired to lift Native Americans and Black Americans out of their poverty through education, and Servant of God Nicholas Black Elk, who sought to hold onto his Lakota culture while teaching the Catholic faith, help us to acknowledge the challenges of being educators and catechists who respect the dignity of all persons.

WHAT CAN WE LEARN FROM ST. KATHARINE DREXEL AND SERVANT OF GOD NICHOLAS BLACK ELK?

I'm grateful to St. Katharine Drexel and Servant of God Nicholas Black Elk for dedicating their lives to the education and faith development of those that the Church has often neglected. Their examples can help us remember to look for ways to lift up all our students.

- *Seek help from spiritual advisors.* When she wanted to know how to help poor Native and Black Americans, Katharine sought counsel from the pope and other bishops, who persuaded her to start a missionary order dedicated to education. If you see an injustice in your school or parish community, seek out the advice of those in authority and those in a position to help. Yes, they might just tell you to take care of it yourself, as Pope Leo XIII told Katharine, but it was the combined counsel of three men that convinced her to do the work.
- *Remember where you came from.* Nicholas Black Elk found ways to integrate faith and culture. He used that to his advantage when teaching other Native Americans about Christ. This is culturally

relevant pedagogy in action. Do we consider ways to make our own teaching culturally relevant to our students?

Teach Parents, Too: St. Dulce Lopes Pontes

Maria Rita de Souza Brito Lopes Pontes (1914–1992) was born to an upper-middle-class family in Brazil. As a girl she would often visit the slums with her aunt, and at the age of thirteen, she had a life-changing experience that left her with a strong desire to serve the poor. Thus, she joined the Missionary Sisters of the Immaculate Conception after high school and took her late mother's name, Dulce.

Her first job was teaching geography. Later, Irmã (Sister) Dulce taught reading and writing to the poor in the slums. She taught the children during the day and their parents at night. So intent was she on lifting people up through education that she spent her lunch breaks looking for people to teach about the faith and how to read.

By age twenty-two, Irmã Dulce had already started a Catholic workers' organization to support the working poor. Years later, she established a school for workers and their children. She also founded the Charitable Works Foundation of Sister Dulce, one of the largest organizations of its kind in Brazil.

Irmã Dulce invested in her own education as well. She trained as a teacher and a nurse and even completed a pharmacy course. She was also brave and creative. In order to care for more people, she asked her religious order if she could use the convent's chicken yard to create a hostel. She was given permission as long as she took care of the chickens, which she agreed to do. However, her idea of taking care of the chickens was to feed them to the guests of the hostel! Her bravery came into play when a bus crashed outside the convent. Irmã Dulce climbed on a crate, broke a window, and pulled people from the burning vehicle.

WHAT CAN WE LEARN FROM ST. DULCE LOPES PONTES?

I love that Dulce didn't just teach the poor children; she took time to teach their parents as well. Our kids' parents can be even more eager to learn than their children. What adult-education opportunities or resources does your school offer?

- *Help parents help their children.* I've worked at schools that have held some awesome education nights for parents, ranging from internet safety to English-language learning. When my own school can't provide educational sessions for parents, I've directed them to the local public library or organizations that help refugees and immigrants.
- *Eliminate barriers to parent-teacher communications.* I once had a parent come to a conference with an adult child who acted as a translator. The adult daughter said her mom wanted to know where she could take classes to learn better English. By helping the parents, we can sometimes pave the way to enrich our students' learning as well.

Fight for What's Right: Venerable Mary Elizabeth Lange

Mary Elizabeth Lange (1789–1882) was born to a wealthy Haitian family that fled to Cuba just before the Haitian Revolution. In 1813, she and her mom moved to the United States. Her mom eventually returned to Cuba, but Mary Elizabeth stayed in Baltimore, Maryland, which was a slave state. Despite her wealth and education (she spoke French, Spanish, and English), she faced discrimination in the Church and society. In the 1820s, she decided to use her family's wealth to start a school for free Black children in Baltimore. Unfortunately, the school closed in 1827 when she ran out of funding.

Mary Elizabeth wanted to join a religious order, but no white order of religious sisters would accept her. Then she met Fr. James Hector Joubert, a French Sulpician priest. Frustrated by his inability to catechize his illiterate parishioners, he knew his job would be easier if they could read, so he helped Mary Elizabeth found the Oblate Sisters of Providence. Hers was the first successful order for African American women, and they devoted themselves to caring for Black people, especially through education. The order founded a school for girls of color forty years before the Emancipation Proclamation was signed.

After Fr. Joubert died and funding ran out, the bishop of Baltimore wanted to disband the order, but Mary Elizabeth and her sisters took on odd jobs, such as laundry, cooking, and cleaning, to pay the bills. They survived despite the anti-Catholic violence of the Know-Nothing Party, the Civil War, and its aftermath. They even started a program to train teachers and a night school for adults. They offered vocational training, spiritual direction, and catechism classes. Through all this, they endured ridicule and physical threats from both racist white Catholics and anti-Catholics.

WHAT CAN WE LEARN FROM VENERABLE MARY ELIZABETH LANGE?

Mary Elizabeth Lange's courage and determination inspire me. She could have given up so many times for many different reasons, but she didn't. Let's ask her to pray for us when we feel like throwing in the towel.

- *Don't let the naysayers stop you.* I can only imagine the vitriol Mary Elizabeth must have faced. People hated her for her skin color, her faith, or both! Even within her own Church, she faced racism. None of this stopped her, though, because she knew children needed her help. She could have used her own wealth to live a fairly comfortable life, but she didn't. She could have given up when the money ran out, but she didn't. She could have caved when Fr. Joubert died and the bishop of Baltimore wanted to end things, but she didn't. Instead of looking inward and feeling sorry for herself, she looked outward, toward the families that needed her, and she left a lasting legacy.

- *Dream big.* In a state where slavery existed, Mary Elizabeth's goal of founding a school for free Black children must have seemed impossible to achieve. Do you hope for changes in your school that seem like a pipe dream? While discussing a change I hoped would occur at a school, a teacher once told me, "That will never happen here!" Perhaps she's right, but maybe she's not. We can't give up on our big dreams for our schools and our students. Mary Elizabeth Lange didn't give up on her dream of a school for children of color even after facing extreme racism. We can't give up either.

Saint Squad Summary: Create a Future for Everyone

I've been blessed to speak numerous times at the C3 Conference for the Archdiocese of Los Angeles, an education conference for Catholic school and parish employees. One summer the keynote speaker was Jesuit priest Gregory Boyle. He's the founder of Homeboy Industries, the largest gang-intervention, rehabilitation, and reentry program in the world.

Instead of a lengthy talk, Fr. Greg spoke briefly and then introduced a woman from Homeboy Industries. Her story of how "G" (as many of these former gang members call Fr. Greg) found her and gave her training and a job brought tears to many eyes. Lives are transformed when people are given the opportunity to be properly trained so that they can support themselves through honest work.

After the talk, I received a signed copy of Fr. Greg's book *The Whole Language*. In the introduction, he quotes Pope Francis as saying, "The only future worth building includes everyone."[5] Isn't that what many of the saints in this chapter were trying to do—create a future that includes everyone? Isn't that what we try to do as educators?

Particularly in recent centuries, many in the Church have fought for an education for everyone. Education used to be only for the rich, but many priests, brothers, and sisters worked to provide education for the poor. At a time when girls weren't educated beyond caring for the home, saints stepped up to include girls in education at all levels. When people of color were denied education or sent to segregated schools with inferior resources, more saints stepped up to include them.

Today there is much talk about making our schools (both public and private) more inclusive. Recently, I read a beautiful news story about students at a public grade school in Minnesota who saw their classmates in wheelchairs sitting on the sidelines during recess because none of the playground equipment was accessible to them. The fifth graders led a series of fundraisers so they could buy the adaptive equipment themselves. After months of hard work, they raised the $300,000 necessary to make their playground more inclusive and started making plans to raise money for other schools in their district to do the same.

Let the children lead the way.

REFLECTION QUESTIONS

1. St. Charles Lwanga protected young boys from a predator king. How can you keep a watchful eye out for students who might be suffering from abuse? We won't purge our Church, our schools, or our society of this evil without a concerted effort from everyone.
2. St. Katharine Drexel sought advice from wise counselors. When you see an injustice, whose help might you seek out?

3. Servant of God Nicholas Black Elk used cultural ties to teach the faith. How have you considered your cultural background as well as those of your students when deciding the best ways to teach?

4. St. Dulce Lopes Pontes made sure to teach the parents, too. Does your school offer educational programs for parents? Or are there community programs you can recommend?

5. Venerable Mary Elizabeth Lange didn't take no for an answer. When have you ignored the naysayers and pushed onward?

SIX

Saints Who Surpassed Expectations

It is not necessary to have been well-educated, to have spent many years in college, to love the good God. It is sufficient to want to do so generously.

—St. André Bessette

Did you know that some saints were actually terrible students? Most of their teachers and classmates never suspected these low achievers would end up being influential members of the Church, much less saints. But isn't that God's way? He exalts the lowly!

Notice your Quiet Students: St. Thomas Aquinas

Thomas Aquinas (1225–1274) is considered one of the most brilliant minds and greatest philosophers of the Catholic Church. He is the patron saint of Catholic universities, scholars, students, schools, and theologians. In 1567, Pope Pius V declared him a Doctor of the Church.

Despite all this, as a student Thomas Aquinas was labeled "the dumb ox"! At an early age, Thomas was attracted to the Dominicans. When he expressed the desire to join them, his family protested. The Dominicans were seen as beggars, and his family thought that way of life was beneath them. If he wanted to join a religious order, they preferred that he join the Benedictines because he would at least have a chance of becoming abbot at the prestigious Monte Cassino. His brothers went so far as to imprison him in a castle and send a prostitute to tempt him in order to get him to change his mind.

Eventually, Thomas studied at the University of Paris. Since he was such a quiet student, his classmates mistook his silence for a lack of intelligence, hence "the dumb ox" nickname. However, St. Albert the Great, under whom Thomas studied, saw his potential and predicted that the "lowing of this dumb ox would be heard all over the world."[1] Other faculty members and classmates didn't take notice of Thomas until he began to teach and preach. They marveled at how he used Aristotle's ideas to explain Christian beliefs, bringing together philosophy and theology. He ended up spending two decades teaching and writing in Paris and Italy.

WHAT CAN WE LEARN FROM ST. THOMAS AQUINAS?

During my undergraduate studies at Marquette University, I was required to take a literary criticism class. That's a perfectly logical requirement for someone studying to become an English teacher.

However, the very idea of "literary criticism" seemed foreign to me. I read literature for fun. Why did I need to criticize it? Uncomfortable with the notion of literary criticism, I sat through many classes never daring to say a word. Other students dominated the conversation as I listened and took notes. In the second half of the semester, we each had to lead a mini-lesson on one of the required readings. I had no problem with that. I did theater in high school. I came in third in a speech contest in junior high. I was a lector at church. Getting up and speaking in front of a crowd has always come fairly naturally to me despite my shy nature.

When I received my classmates' feedback forms, there were several comments to the effect of "Where has this girl been all semester? Her talk was great, but I didn't even realize she was in the class until now," and "This was great. Informative and well delivered! Wish she shared her ideas more in class."

St. Thomas Aquinas, I feel ya!

- *Don't underestimate the quiet ones.* Like St. Thomas Aquinas and me, some students need time to process their ideas before they share them. Give us time to write out our thoughts first, or let us discuss them with a peer before we talk in front of the whole class. This is probably why "think, pair, share" became such a popular teaching device. Some of us want a moment to think first and then have our ideas validated by a peer before we are brave enough to talk in front of a group.
- *Don't underestimate your value as a mentor.* I wonder how much Thomas shared with St. Albert before he began teaching and preaching. What words of advice did St. Albert give him? While I don't know much about their relationship, I do know that St. Albert believed in him, and I know that our students need us to believe in them, too. It only takes one of us to make a difference. The other faculty members didn't see Thomas's potential right away, but St. Albert did.

Revel in Humble Doorkeepers: St. André Bessette and Bl. Solanus Casey

I confess I often mix up St. André Bessette and Bl. Solanus Casey because their stories are quite similar, and their giftedness is cloaked in humility—the post of doorkeeper was typically not given to a member of the order with recognized scholarly abilities. And yet, these two men had other, hidden gifts for which they were remembered long after their deaths. Let's take a look at them both.

André Bessette (1845–1937) was born to a poor family in Quebec. He was plagued with sickness from birth (the midwife baptized him immediately because he was so weak) and orphaned by age twelve. Before his mom died, she tried to teach him to write his name and read a little. His brothers attempted to teach him more later, but he always read with difficulty. Over the course of thirteen years, he undertook many jobs (blacksmith, baker, factory worker), but his poor health made it hard, and he failed at each one.

When André was twenty-five, a priest friend helped him become a brother of the Congregation of Holy Cross, where he did simple jobs, such as washing floors and windows, cleaning lamps, carrying firewood, and delivering messages. Eventually, he was asked to be the doorkeeper of Notre Dame College in Montreal. With his typical good sense of humor, he said, "My superiors showed me the door, and I stayed there forty years."[2]

When André greeted sick people at the door, he encouraged them to pray novenas to St. Joseph and to wear St. Joseph medals. He also anointed them with oil from a lamp that burned before St. Joseph's image in the monastery. Many of these people received miraculous healings. From 1910 to 1937, ten thousand people were healed, about one a day. During one year, 435 cures were reported.

André persuaded his superiors to build a small chapel to St. Joseph, which eventually became the Oratory of St. Joseph, now the largest shrine to St. Joseph in the world. When André died at age ninety-one, at least one million people passed his coffin lying in state over the course of a week. The media called him the "Miracle Worker of Montreal" and the "Saint of Mount Royale."[3]

Bl. Solanus Casey (1870–1957) had a similar profession with similar results. Bernard Francis Casey was the sixth of sixteen children born to Irish immigrant parents. Growing up in Wisconsin, he was a mediocre student who struggled so much in the diocesan seminary that they kicked him out. He became a Capuchin monk and took the name Francis Solanus. In 1904, he was ordained a "simplex priest," meaning that he could not celebrate Mass or hear Confession.

Over the next twenty years, Solanus spent time doing simple jobs in Capuchin monasteries in New York until he was made a doorkeeper. People soon came to him seeking his good counsel. Later he was moved to Detroit, Michigan, where he continued working as a doorkeeper and listening to people's problems. As with St. André, many miracles occurred when Solanus prayed. In 1921, he was put in charge of enrolling people in the Seraphic Mass Association. Capuchins all over the world pray for these people at daily Mass. By 1923, so many healings had occurred that the Capuchins told Solanus to keep a log. When he died at age eighty-six, twenty thousand people walked past his casket over the course of a day and a half.

WHAT CAN WE LEARN FROM ST. ANDRÉ BESSETTE AND BL. SOLANUS CASEY?

They may not have been traditional educators, but St. André and Bl. Solanus can teach us some important lessons about our students. Consider who in your classroom might not be on the honor roll but has a great deal of social and emotional intelligence and knows how to listen well and respond with good counsel.

- *College degrees aren't the only path to success.* Not all of our students will be successful in school, yet God has a plan for them to contribute positively to this world. Yes, I value education, but sometimes I think we educators put too much importance on academics. People with advanced degrees can be let go from jobs if they have terrible people skills. Conversely, I know many hard workers with good people skills and common sense who started their own successful companies despite not having a college degree. St. André and Bl. Solanus didn't need advanced degrees to become saints—or to make a lasting difference to the thousands who came to them for counsel.

- *Listen with humility, compassion, and wisdom.* Why did so many people come to these two humble doorkeepers? They listened to others in a way that radiated God's love. Neither was "book smart," yet they were wise in the ways of the world and in their way of receiving others with an open ear and a welcoming heart.

Early in my career, I often worried about having all the right answers. Years of making tons of small mistakes (Why is it I can misspell words on the board and not realize it until I take three steps back? Or proofread a test twenty times and still not catch every typo?) has taught me that those simple human failings aren't what matter most in this world—or even in our classrooms. What matters is how I relate to my students. Do I listen to them when they are crying out for help (often manifested as poor behavior)? And do I answer with humility and wisdom so that they see me as someone to whom they can turn when they need assistance?

Help English-Language Learners: St. Bernadette Soubirous

For most people, St. Bernadette Soubirous (1844–1879) needs little introduction. You may already know the story of her encounter with Our Lady of Lourdes, and her discovery of the healing waters at Lourdes, France. But did you know she struggled with learning as a child?

Bernadette was the oldest daughter of a poor miller in Lourdes. When her father lost the mill, the family moved into a 10 × 10-foot room that had previously been a prison.

In 1857, Bernadette was sent to Bartrès to study with her "foster mother," Marie Lagues. She was supposed to go to school and learn her catechism, but Marie sent her to watch the sheep instead. Marie did try to teach Bernadette her catechism at night, but the text was written in formal French, and Bernadette was only familiar with her own dialect. This language barrier made it impossible for Bernadette to learn her lessons. Without them, she could not make her first Communion. After two years of trying and failing, Bernadette was sent home. She simply couldn't master formal French.

This is what makes Bernadette's experiences with Our Lady of Lourdes so remarkable. Mary appeared to Bernadette in the grotto multiple times. On the day of the thirteenth apparition, more than 1,500 people came with her. Afterward, Bernadette told the local pastor, Abbé Peyramale, that the lady said, "Go, tell the priests to come here in procession and build a chapel house."[4] The priest told Bernadette to ask the lady her name and, because he was skeptical, to make a rosebush in the grotto bloom.

When Mary next appeared, Bernadette asked her name. Mary responded (in formal French, rather than the patois Bernadette naturally understood), "I am the Immaculate Conception."[5] Bernadette had to repeat the unfamiliar words to herself over and over on the way to Abbé Peyramale because she did not understand them. Pope Pius IX had declared the dogma of the Immaculate Conception just four years earlier. It wasn't widely known, definitely not something a poor girl in a small town in France would have known and definitely not in formal French! While many people doubted the authenticity of Bernadette's claims at first, her report of the lady's name made it hard to keep doubting her. There was no way this poorly educated girl, who knew only her own dialect, could have come up with the new Marian appellation all on her own.

WHAT CAN WE LEARN FROM ST. BERNADETTE SOUBIROUS?

When I get a new English speaker in my classroom, I always think of my father, who spoke only Italian when he started school. When his English-language skills were still low at the end of first grade, the Chicago public schools decided he needed to repeat the grade. Thankfully, much has improved in the way English-language learners (ELLs) are treated nowadays. How does St. Bernadette's story speak to you about the needs of these children?

- *Lack of language skills doesn't mean lack of intelligence.* Some of my brightest students have been ones who have struggled with language issues. Their natural gifts and abilities can easily remain dormant as they struggle to make sense of their new environment. How you treat these children provides a powerful example to your other students, teaching them lessons in compassion and patience.

- *Some kinds of language take longer to acquire.* General conversational skills for a new language can be picked up within a year or so. However, it can take seven to nine years for students to develop academic language skills (such as discipline-specific vocabulary and the language skills necessary to handle standardized tests) so that they are on par with native speakers.[6] Often, I've had to remind myself that students who seem fluent in English can still stumble over words like *compare* and *contrast* or *antonyms* and *synonyms*. Consider what kind of academic language or content-specific terminology might need more explanation for your ELL population.

Create Effective Accommodations: Bl. Carlos Manuel Rodríguez Santiago

Carlos Manuel Rodríguez Santiago (1918–1963) was the first Puerto Rican, first Caribbean born, and first layperson in US history to be beatified. Like St. Thomas Aquinas, he was not known for being a great scholar in his younger years but went on to become an important teacher.

In his youth, Carlos rescued a cousin from a dog attack. The stress of that situation may be the reason he suffered from ulcerative colitis, which caused him to drop out of high school. Despite this, he read avidly and eventually earned his diploma at the age of twenty-one. He tried to attend a university with the hope of becoming a priest, but once again his ill health made him drop out.

Carlos taught high school catechism, translated the Mass prayers from Latin to Spanish so people could understand the liturgy better, and used his own meager income to publish prayers and articles in his own magazines: *Liturgy* and *Christian Culture*. Eventually, he quit his office clerk job to teach liturgy classes at the University of Puerto Rico's Catholic student center.

Carlos lived a simple life of service, owning only one pair of shoes and playing the organ at Mass after only one year of piano lessons. He passionately advocated for the Easter Vigil to return to the Saturday evening before Easter (at the time, it was being celebrated earlier on Holy Saturday) and for the use of the vernacular and more lay participation during Mass.

WHAT CAN WE LEARN FROM BL. CARLOS MANUEL RODRÍGUEZ SANTIAGO?

Carlos did not give up on learning when illness prevented him from going to school, but he did change his approach to learning. He had to read on his own, and thus it took him much longer to earn his diploma. Very often as teachers we are asked to make accommodations for

students with health issues. But how often do we stop to consider that
in doing so we might be helping a future saint?

- *Consider how you regard students with specific needs.* As teachers
  we are frequently asked to accommodate the needs of students
  for health reasons: the diabetics who need to monitor their blood
  sugar level or eat snacks during class, the hearing impaired who
  need us to wear a lanyard with a special mic and turn on the
  closed captioning for videos, or the visually impaired who need
  to sit in the front and use texts with larger print. When you have
  to do these things, do you do them joyfully—or with resentment?

  Confession time: Sometimes I get overwhelmed with the vast
  array of accommodations we must make. It's not that I don't think
  they are necessary or helpful; it just gets challenging, especially
  if you see more than a hundred students every day and dozens of
  them have different needs. Who gets extra test time? Who needs
  tests read to them? Who needs to check in with the nurse? Who
  has which allergies? (And why are there so many more than when
  I started teaching?) Did I remember to find the video with the
  closed captioning?

  When the stress overcomes me, I'm thankful to have Bl.
  Carlos on my saint squad. He can remind me of the holiness of
  the work we do when we meet our students' individual learning
  needs.

- *Be thankful when your efforts produce good fruit.* One year, on
  our annual Shakespeare-play field trip, a student needed a special listening device to hear the actors, and one of my coworkers
  who had recently returned from maternity leave asked me to
  check with the theater to see if they had a space she could use as
  a lactation room. Multiple emails and phone calls ensued, but
  thankfully, the Chicago Shakespeare Theater company was very
  accommodating on both accounts.

The extra effort paid off: My coworker was very appreciative, and
the hearing-impaired student's mom thanked me multiple times for
helping her son to enjoy the play. These are the kinds of things we

often aren't prepped for during our teacher-education courses, but they are so important—and the story of Bl. Carlos Manuel Rodríguez Santiago reminds us that taking care of these students (and sometimes our coworkers!) shouldn't feel like a burden but good and holy work.

Saint Squad Summary: Find the Hidden Genius (or Saint!) Right in Front of You

The secular world is full of examples of people who seemed like failures at first. Steven Spielberg was rejected from film school. Albert Einstein's speech development was much slower than that of the typical child, and he was told by a teacher that he would never amount to anything. Thomas Edison did so poorly in a traditional school that he only stayed for a few months before being homeschooled by his mom.

I wonder what my dad's first-grade teacher thought when she insisted he repeat first grade. Did she think he would always be behind? Did she know that he actually skipped a grade later? Could she even imagine he would become the first in his family to go to college, much less receive an industrial engineering degree from the prestigious program at the University of Illinois?

Sometimes we can see a child's potential early on, but often we really don't know what course our students' lives will take. God may have something completely unexpected and surprising in store for them. And even if I can't see the genius or the saint right in front of me, God can.

REFLECTION QUESTIONS

1. St. Albert the Great saw the brilliance in St. Thomas Aquinas.
    How can you give your quieter students opportunities to shine?
2. St. André Bessette and Bl. Solanus Casey listened to people's needs
    with humility, compassion, and wisdom. How can you do the
    same for your students?
3. St. Bernadette's foster mother did not exercise patience with her
    as she struggled to learn formal French. How have you recognized
    the gifts of your English-language learners while supporting their
    language-learning efforts?
4. Bl. Carlos needed to learn in his own time and in his own way.
    How have some of your students needed creative accommoda-
    tions? Have you seen this as a burden or as a chance to serve
    humbly?

SEVEN

Saints Who Taught in Times of Crisis

When our hearts are reluctant, we often have to compel ourselves to pray for our enemies, to pour out prayer for those who are against us. Would that our hearts were filled with love!

—St. Gregory the Great

As I began researching this book at the tail end of the COVID-19 pandemic, I found it comforting to know that many of the teacher saints I encountered were no strangers to educating during times of crisis and confusion. During the pandemic, the word "unprecedented" had been thrown around so often, it was easy to forget that chaos and confusion occur in every age. It's all about how we weather the storm.

In this chapter, we'll look at five saints who lived and taught during times of catastrophe and chaos. Each of them taught me a lesson in how to handle the storms I encounter as an educator.

Use the Skills You've Been Given: Bl. Miguel Pro

If you've seen the movie *For Greater Glory*, you know the chaos, confusion, and downright terror priests experienced in Mexico at the time Miguel Agustín Pro Juárez (1891–1927) lived. During the Mexican Revolution (1910–1917), anticlerical laws forbade men from entering the seminary. In 1926, President Plutarco Elías Calles enacted laws that made it illegal for priests to do their work. Foreign-born priests were killed or sent back to their home countries. Native-born priests who celebrated the sacraments or wore their clericals in public were jailed, shot, or hanged. It was during these terrifying times that Miguel Pro became a Jesuit priest.

You probably know the Jesuits for their many high schools and universities, but did you know that every Jesuit scholastic (a Jesuit who is studying for the priesthood) must spend three years actively working in a ministry, usually teaching at a high school or college or engaged in campus ministry? Imagine being a first-year teacher right after fleeing your home country to avoid imprisonment. This is exactly what Miguel Pro did.

Miguel was studying to become a Jesuit at the start of the Mexican Revolution. When the government outlawed religious formation, the rector of Miguel's seminary sent the young men out in small groups, dressed in street clothes, to escape. Posing as a servant in peasant's clothes, Pro made his way to Texas and then California. Over the next few years, he continued his studies as he found his way to Nicaragua, Spain, and eventually Belgium. It was during this time of constant movement that he began his work as a teacher.

As I write this, I think of a Jesuit scholastic whom I've befriended on Instagram. He is just starting his three years of teaching at a Cristo Rey high school in Chicago. I don't envy him learning how to teach during a national teacher shortage. It's hard enough for me as a veteran teacher! However, I know he's a fan of Miguel Pro, and I can't think of a better saint squad member for anyone starting their teaching career during challenging times.

Things didn't get easier for Miguel after he became a priest in 1925. He suffered from stomach pains that various operations did not help. Believing he needed a diet of more familiar foods, the priests in Belgium sent him back to his homeland in 1926. Unfortunately, just twenty-three days later, President Calles banned public worship and began arresting and killing priests who said Mass.

How did Fr. Miguel persevere through this next set of trials? He used some skills and talents from his younger years when he was known to be a bit of a prankster and an actor. Prior to his decision to become a Jesuit, Miguel had visited family friends who were Jesuit missionaries in another town. One day, he swiped a cassock and headed out to the countryside, pretending to preach. He was so convincing that those who heard him gave him gifts of eggs, cheese, and cigarettes.[1] When the Jesuits found out, they relieved Miguel of his bounty but took no further action, since nothing he had preached had been contrary to the truth.

Later, as an actual Jesuit, Miguel's acting talents proved useful as he donned a variety of disguises to escape imprisonment. Dressed as a mechanic, he preached to chauffeurs. Disguised as a police officer, he visited priests in jails. Clothed as a beggar, he went virtually unnoticed on the streets as he moved from neighborhood to neighborhood secretly saying weddings, hearing Confessions, and collecting food for the poor. He would even pretend to be meeting a girlfriend as he set up spots where the faithful could clandestinely receive Communion.

In addition to his acting talents, Miguel's innate fearlessness helped him operate under this repressive regime. As a toddler, he once crept away from his nursemaid and climbed out on a window ledge, where his terrified mother later found him crawling three stories above a busy street. This fearlessness came in handy years later when he had to leap from a moving taxi in order to avoid capture.

Eventually, Miguel and one of his brothers were falsely accused of throwing a bomb in a car belonging to an ally of President Calles. The president boasted that he had killed fifty priests himself, and now he vowed to make a public mockery of Fr. Miguel. President Calles brought in reporters to watch Miguel's execution, hoping that the image of a priest begging for his life would curb members of the Cristero Rebellion, who had risen up in response to the banning of Catholicism in Mexico.

The president didn't count on Miguel's courage. As he was led to his execution, Miguel remained quiet and only asked for a moment to pray so that he could forgive the police officer who had asked for pardon. Then he spread his arms wide as if on a cross and cried, "Viva Cristo Rey!" ("Long live Christ the King!") as he was shot by a firing squad.[2] Instead of dissuading further rebellion, Miguel's execution strengthened the resolve of the Catholics in Mexico. Though public demonstrations were forbidden, Miguel's funeral procession consisted of five hundred cars, and tens of thousands of admirers lined the streets.

WHAT CAN WE LEARN FROM BL. MIGUEL PRO?

Bl. Miguel's courage astounds me. I've had to endure some dangerous times in my teaching career (e.g., fire in the building, bomb threat, lockdown because of an escaped, armed criminal in the neighborhood), but this all seems to pale in comparison to Miguel's experiences.

During times of crisis, it can be easy to let our emotions overwhelm us. Instead of giving in to anxiety and despair, Miguel used his talents to continue preaching.

Before we get into the specific tips, I'll share one example from my own career. I completed my doctorate while teaching full-time. The hours were grueling: fifty hours a week teaching, plus 2½-hour classes (sometimes two or three per week), plus homework. In order to survive, I took things one day at a time with lots of careful planning, to-do lists, and rewarding myself in small ways when I finished a task.

When the COVID-19 pandemic hit, I was writing up the findings of my dissertation research. During those first months of the stay-at-home orders, I thought nothing could be harder than trying to reinvent education as we know it while simultaneously writing my dissertation and my first book for teachers. I was wrong. The next two years of teaching were even harder. I survived by using what I had learned while completing my doctorate as a full-time teacher. They are the same things Bl. Miguel Pro modeled for us:

- *Take things one day at a time.* Miguel didn't know from one day to the next if he'd be arrested. He just kept preaching anyway. During COVID, I didn't know if I would be quarantined from one day to the next or even which students would be in my classroom versus on Zoom. I just kept teaching anyway. Taking things one day at a time has helped me continue as we face the fallout from the pandemic.
- *Set little goals.* I imagine Miguel didn't have an elaborate plan for his disguises. He decided which disguise to use based on where he needed to go that day. It's easy for us as teachers to be over-whelmed by all the standards and goals we need to meet by the end of the year. It's good to have the end goal in sight, but once you've outlined your approach, take each school day as it comes.
- *Celebrate when you can.* In the midst of thousands of villagers being killed, Miguel still celebrated weddings and baptisms. At times when I've felt my coworkers needed a pick-me-up, I've brought in donuts to celebrate making it to Friday. Don't forget to take time to celebrate with your students, too! When they've hit a milestone, find a way to mark it with a fun activity or class-room reward.

Keep Calm and Carry On: Bl. Peter To Rot

Peter To Rot (1912–1945) was born in Rakunai, New Britain, an island village in what is now called Papua New Guinea. The Missionaries of Charity had been working there since 1882, and by 1898 many of the

people—including Peter's mother Maria and father Angelo, chief of
the Rakunai village—had converted to Catholicism.

When Peter was young, his father taught him the basics of the
faith. Their parish priest saw how pious Peter was as a child and
encouraged him to become a priest. However, Angelo did not agree
to this, so Peter settled for training as a catechist, which he began in
1930 at age eighteen.

In 1936, Peter married Paula la Varpit, with whom he had three
children. Peter and Paula often prayed together, and two of their children traveled with Peter as he catechized the villagers. He organized
both large and small group instruction and prayer. His teaching was
straightforward, immediate, and effective as he worked to get to know
the people and their problems. He carried a Bible with him at all times
and often quoted from it during lessons.

Unfortunately, life on the island changed drastically when the
Japanese invaded in 1942. The missionaries and mission staff were
sent to concentration camps; priests were arrested and put in jail.
Peter became a spiritual leader of his people. He held secret prayer services, catechesis classes, and Communion services (he would smuggle
consecrated hosts out of the jails after visiting priests). When his
village church was destroyed, Peter built a secret place to worship,
hidden by tree branches.

When the Japanese decided that the island people should return
to the old practice of polygamy, which they had abandoned after the
first Protestant missionaries arrived fifty years earlier, Peter spoke
out against it. In 1945, Peter was arrested and eventually executed
by lethal injection.

WHAT CAN WE LEARN FROM BL. PETER TO ROT?

While I've never had to teach under foreign occupation, there are
times when we are called to speak truth in difficult situations. Bl.
Peter To Rot's example can give us guidance for handling worst-case
scenarios.

- *Keep that Bible handy!* Peter traveled with a Bible as he moved about his village to teach the faith. I'm sure it must have been a source of comfort during times of struggle. Need a spiritual boost? Try reading the psalms, especially Psalm 28:6–9:

> Blessed be the Lord,
>   who has heard the sound of my pleading.
> The Lord is my strength and my shield,
>   in whom my heart trusts.
> I am helped, so my heart rejoices;
>   with my song I praise him.
>
> Lord, you are a strength for your people,
>   the saving refuge of your anointed.
> Save your people, bless your inheritance;
>   pasture and carry them forever!

- *Get creative.* Peter built a makeshift church hidden by trees so as to avoid detection by the Japanese. When we were forced into online learning, I found creative ways to turn my old worksheets into online games such as Kahoot!, Quizizz, Blooket, and Quizlet. It was so successful that I continued to use these games even after we returned to the classroom and could pass out paper again. Bonus to this creative solution: less photocopying!
- *Seek help from spiritual advisors.* When the priests were jailed, Peter visited them. He probably had dual motives: having the priests consecrate hosts he smuggled into the jail and encouraging the priests with news from the village. However, I bet he also received consolation from those visits. I'm grateful for the spiritual directors, priests, and retreat leaders who have fed my soul over the years.

Leave Behind a Legacy: St. Gertrude the Great

Gertrude the Great (1256–1302) lived in the midst of violence and chaos. From 1250 to 1273, military conflicts waged between the Holy Roman Emperor and the pope and between the feudal lords and the town leaders. In the midst of this conflict, Gertrude was orphaned at a young age and raised at a Benedictine abbey in Germany. At the monastery school, she studied Latin grammar, rhetoric, and the writings of the church fathers. It's possible she also studied arithmetic, astronomy, geometry, and music. As a young woman, she loved studying so much that she would shorten her prayer time so that she could spend more time in the library . . . until Jesus appeared to her and told her that her studying was coming between them. (Don't we wish some of our students had half of St. Gertrude's love of studying?)

Gertrude began to focus more on Jesus and his Sacred Heart. She wrote down her reflections and conversations with Jesus so that she could share them with others. In fact, she wrote several books; one is a compilation of several shorter pieces she had written on her visions and others' stories. She also wrote a book on meditation and prayer, now known as *The Exercises of St. Gertrude*.

As a teacher, Gertrude prepared simplified versions of the writings of the church fathers so that beginners could read and understand them, and she improved the monastery's library. Gertrude managed to keep busy teaching and writing while the leaders of the world and the Church waged war against one another.

Gertrude's writings were so insightful that they were translated into Latin and French during the sixteenth and seventeenth centuries. They influenced saints such as Teresa of Ávila, Philip Neri, and Francis de Sales. Her secret to perseverance? She believed that trusting in God would bring us confidence in ourselves.

WHAT CAN WE LEARN FROM ST. GERTRUDE THE GREAT?

St. Gertrude is proof that even if it seems like lawlessness is taking over our world, we can still persevere in our work as educators.

- *Trust in God!* He has a plan for us, even in the midst of chaos. Sometimes it feels like I should be doing something "bigger" with my life, but St. Gertrude had the right idea. When I feel powerless to radically change "the system"—including how others vote, or what elected officials do once they are in office—I *can* keep working toward educating my students so that they will make wise choices when it's their turn to lead.
- *Meet people where they are.* Gertrude prepared simplified versions of the church fathers' writings so that more people would have access to them. This makes me think of hi-lo books: high-interest books with lower Lexile levels to provide older, struggling students with reading material that isn't too immature for them. When circumstances beyond our control put our students behind academically, we can lift them up by meeting them where they are. We can't expect them to jump up to the level we think is appropriate; sometimes we have to simplify our lessons before we can bridge the gap.

Step Up to the Plate: St. Gregory the Great

Gregory the Great (540–604) was the son of a Roman senator who passed on to him a sense of civic responsibility. The Roman Empire had fallen, and the great city of Rome was mostly in ruins. Rome had been hit repeatedly by plagues, natural disasters, and invasions from the Goths and Lombards. Gregory managed to finish his classical education just before the schools closed.

When he was only thirty, Gregory became the prefect of Rome, and he was greatly admired for how he handled the administration of the city. However, he did not want a life in politics. In 573, he sold his property, gave his money to the poor, and opened seven monasteries, one of which he joined in 574. He loved the contemplative life and wanted to remain in the monastery, but God had other plans. First, he was called to be one of the seven deacons of Rome. Then Pope Pelagius II made him ambassador to the imperial court in Constantinople.

In 590, when Pope Pelagius died during one of the plague outbreaks, the people and the emperor wanted Gregory as pope. He felt unworthy but was elected anyway. Because the civil administration of Rome (and much of the surrounding area) was crumbling, Gregory had to deal with famine, plague, and multiple attacks from outsiders.

During his thirteen years as pope, Gregory taught the faith through his writing and his preaching. In his homilies, he used stories to get his points across. He reformed monasteries and the liturgies, and codified music into what we now call Gregorian chant. His writings on church fathers such as St. Augustine and his commentaries on the Bible made these works accessible to all. His works include *Dialogues* (a book on the lives of holy men) and *Pastoral Care*. Throughout all this, his anxiety caused him to suffer from gastritis and colitis, yet he persevered and left behind a lasting legacy.

WHAT CAN WE LEARN FROM ST. GREGORY THE GREAT?

When I was young, I considered several careers. With my love of reading and writing, the quiet life of an author seemed appealing. (Little did I know that authors are often also public speakers!) Gregory also dreamed of a quiet life, but just like you and me, God gave him certain gifts suited to teaching, and so he was drawn out of his quiet life to lead the Church during turbulent times.

- *Sometimes you have to lead even when you don't want to.* I never wanted to run the student council. I hadn't even *been* on my grade school's student council, but in my fifth year of teaching, suddenly

I was running the student council. Why? Because nobody else wanted to! We've all been there as educators. Some task needs to be done, no one wants to do it, but eventually you step up because you realize how much it will benefit the kids. I think this is why Gregory finally gave in. He knew God was calling him to use his gifts for the good of the Church. The next time you find yourself in that unexpected leadership position at school, I pray St. Gregory the Great gives you the extra inspiration you need to tackle that job.

- *Pray for those who persecute you.* I started this chapter with a quote from St. Gregory, that our hearts need to be filled with love even for those who might be causing us pain. All the saints in this chapter faced enemies. At some point, we have all been hurt by someone within our schools. If there is someone who comes to mind as an "enemy" right now, remember that St. Gregory's quote is really a reminder of the Sermon on the Mount: "Love your enemies and pray for those who persecute you."

Remember your Calling: Bl. Natalia Tułasiewicz

Natalia Tułasiewicz (1906–1945) was born in Poland to parents who were academic intellectuals. She studied the Polish language and literature as well as philosophy, psychology, and music. In her younger years, she dreamed of being a professional pianist, but when neck surgery left her unable to play at the same level, she turned her dreams toward earning a PhD.

Natalia also dreamed of getting married and became engaged to another intellectual named Janek, but she broke off the engagement because he was an atheist and supported communism. Although she considered joining a religious community, she decided to show her love for Christ by pouring her attention into the high school students she had begun teaching. She loved teaching but hated grading and even referred to it as "a nail in the coffin."[3] Can't we all relate to that? I think a part of me dies every time I have to correct another run-on sentence written by a sixth grader.

Natalia was forced to leave her teaching position when the Nazis invaded Poland and kicked her family out of their home. Moving to Kraków, Natalia worked as a librarian, but she continued to teach secretly as part of the Polish underground. The Nazis were intent on eradicating Polish culture, so Natalia used her secret sessions as a way to keep her country's traditions alive.

When a group of Polish women were sent to work in a labor camp in Germany, Natalia snuck into the group with the intent of continuing her secret teaching. She set up prayer circles, organized a choir, found a priest to give sacraments, and taught Polish, German, and religion to the women in the camp. When the Nazis discovered her activities, they tortured her and then sent her to Ravensbrück concentration camp, where she was sentenced to death.

Natalia taught for the last time on Good Friday in 1945, sharing with the women at the camp about Christ's Passion and Resurrection. The next day, on March 31, she was sent to the gas chamber.

WHAT CAN WE LEARN FROM BL. NATALIA TUŁASIEWICZ?

By pursuing her calling while facing the horrors of a concentration camp, Natalia speaks wisdom to those of us who must deal with far less challenging—though undeniably hostile—work environments.

- *Remember your purpose.* To me, the amazing part of Bl. Natalia's story is that she never lost sight of her purpose. She knew she was meant to teach. When her dream of marriage fell apart, she focused on her teaching. When the Nazis invaded, she found a way to teach secretly. When women were sent into labor camps, she knew they needed someone to keep their hope alive, and she knew that she could offer them strength by occupying their thoughts with learning.

- *Be a source of hope in dark times.* When we are faced with a challenging work environment, let's ask the intercession of Bl. Natalia Tułasiewicz. Let's ask her to remind us that we have been called to teach and despite the harsh conditions we may be given, we can still bring hope to our students.

Saint Squad Summary:
When Hard Times Hit, Use Your Gifts

"If you could have one superpower, what would it be?" I was listening to Fr. Mike Schmitz introduce his talk about working with college students, and his icebreaker question made me stop short. How would you have answered it?

Fr. Mike said he would want the gift of flight, but that answer always leads to him adding on super sight (so he can see better when he flies) and super strength (so he'll be impervious to anything that might impede him). And yet, even then, having powers like Superman wouldn't turn him into Superman. He'd still just be Fr. Mike, but with all these powers. The gifts don't matter as much as how we use them.

Reading all these stories of saints can tempt us to wish for their "superpowers." Why don't I have Bl. Miguel Pro's acting talents? Why don't I have St. Gertrude's trust in God? Our God is generous and will lavish us with gifts, but as Fr. Mike reminded me, we must first be willing to use the gifts we've already been given.

When faced with challenging times, trust that God has already given you the gifts you need. Be generous with those gifts as you work with your students, and God will lavish on you more gifts to help you in your work.

REFLECTION QUESTIONS

1. Bl. Miguel Pro used his acting talents to disguise himself so that he could continue to preach. What gifts has God given you that have helped you be a better teacher?
2. Bl. Peter To Rot sought the help of priests even when they were in prison. What spiritual and educational advisors can you go to when you need a little help?
3. St. Gertrude the Great rewrote the works of the church fathers so her students could understand them. How have you adapted complex materials so that your students can attain greater knowledge and wisdom?
4. God asked St. Gregory the Great to step into leadership positions during challenging times. How is he calling you to lead?
5. Bl. Natalia Tułasiewicz continued to teach even while in a concentration camp. What obstacles have you had to overcome to continue your mission as an educator?

EIGHT

Saints Who Kept Going When the Going Got Tough

Whatever troubles may be before you, accept them cheerfully, remembering whom you are trying to follow. Do not be afraid. Love one another, bear with one another, and let charity guide you in all your life.
—St. Mary MacKillop

Wars, famines, and plagues are certainly times of chaos, but they aren't the only times our teaching jobs get tough. Difficult or absent parents, colleagues with different ideas than our own, and financial challenges can all make teaching hard. Once again, I take comfort in the fact that other educators have faced similar problems and not only lived to tell the tale but became saints in the process.

Trust your Mentors: St. Augustine of Hippo

You probably recognize St. Augustine (354–430) as one of the Doctors of the Church and for his famous work *Confessions*, but did you know he also taught rhetoric and grammar? The story of his life contains many chapters—and yet through all the changes, God placed beacons of faith along the path to guide him toward the good.

Born in the town of Tagaste in North Africa, Augustine was brilliant but undisciplined in his youth. At age seventeen, he went to the university in Carthage to study rhetoric. Focused on worldly goods, success, and desires, he abandoned the Christian faith his mother, St. Monica, had taught him. He also took on a mistress, with whom he had a son when he was only nineteen. He was a strong, prideful student, yet eventually Augustine experienced a dramatic conversion, in part because of his mother's prayers and the influence of holy men who crossed his path as he searched for truth.

As a teacher, Augustine ran his own school for boys where he taught rhetoric and grammar. The boys' lack of discipline upset him so much that he decided to look for better students, moving first to Rome and then to Milan. In Milan, he met St. Ambrose, whom Augustine admired for his eloquence and learning. At age thirty-three he quit teaching, was baptized by Bishop Ambrose, and moved into a home borrowed from a friend to live a simple life of prayer and study with his mom, son, brother, and a few friends.

After Monica died, Augustine returned to Tagaste and lived a monastic life. A few years later, the bishop in Hippo asked Augustine to be his assistant. Reluctant at first to leave the monastery since he felt it would expose him to more temptation, Augustine turned out to be an outstanding preacher. Making use of Bible quotes and anecdotes from real life, he preached so eloquently that he drew hundreds of people. A few years later, Augustine was made bishop of Hippo. He continued to preach even when he became frustrated that people didn't seem to follow his teachings.

Despite his successes, Augustine was plagued with doubt and fears, particularly that he would revert to his former sinful ways. In a letter to St. Jerome, he wrote, "I entreat you again and again to correct me confidently when you perceive me to stand in need of it; for though the office of a bishop be greater than that of a priest, yet in many things Augustine is inferior to Jerome."[1]

WHAT CAN WE LEARN FROM ST. AUGUSTINE OF HIPPO?

Augustine had a lot of people praying for him and helping him out—his mom, St. Ambrose, and St. Jerome, to name a few. Consider for a moment who has mentored and supported you in your work.

- *Find an accountability partner.* Augustine worried that he wasn't good enough, so he asked his friend to let him know if he wasn't living up to his job. Accountability can be a very strong tool, and there's nothing wrong with asking someone to call you out. Some of my coworkers are really good at lifting up women and people of color as role models for students. Every time I see this, I feel inspired to make sure I'm doing the same with the literature I choose and the options I give students for biography research projects. Over the years, I've asked different coworkers to check my list for inclusiveness and diversity. They always come through with great suggestions!
- *The grass isn't always greener on the other side.* You're going to have students who make your job challenging no matter where you teach. As a teacher, Augustine kept moving to different cities—as if he could find a town where the boys would be model students! It can be tempting to think a "better" school would make all our problems disappear. After teaching at eight schools in two states, I've learned this is not the case. While some schools have a more positive atmosphere than others, problems still pop

up. What can you do to make things better, right where you are? Are there mentors who can help you do that?

- *You may be more effective than you think.* When Augustine became a preacher, he was sometimes fed up with people not listening to him any more than his students had! Yet his homilies and writings continue to inspire us today. It's not humanly possible to reach everyone perfectly; just keep teaching anyway. You never know what a difference your words might make—and you could become a mentor for someone else.

Depend on God's Generosity: St. Frances Xavier Cabrini

The first US citizen to be canonized, Francesca Saverio Cabrini (1850–1917) was born in the Lombardy province of Italy. Two months premature, she was so small and weak that her parents feared for her, and illnesses plagued this five-foot-tall saint her whole life. But what she lacked in physical strength she more than made up in spirit.

At a young age, Francesca decided to be a missionary to the East like her hero, the great Jesuit priest St. Francis Xavier (from whom she later took her religious name). She tried to enter two religious orders but was turned down due to her health. Instead, she got her public school teacher's certificate. (Imagine my delight at finding a copy of it hanging in the National Shrine of St. Frances Xavier Cabrini in Chicago.)

At her first teaching job in Vidardo, Francesca won over the students with her gentle yet firm approach. She quickly became known for being humble yet dignified and a great organizer and leader despite her shy nature. When her pastor asked her to run a nearby orphanage for girls in Codogno, she and seven of her students formed the Missionary Sisters of the Sacred Heart of Jesus. At last, Frances believed she was beginning the missionary work she had always desired.

With things well under way in Codogno, Frances traveled to Rome to meet with the cardinal vicar, Msgr. Lucido Parocchi. She had two goals—to start a school in Rome and to get approval for the rule of her order so that it would become a pontifical institute. The cardinal, unsure whether he should lend his support, told Frances to ask God for a sign by procuring five hundred thousand lire for the school.

Instead of being disheartened by the cardinal's lack of enthusiasm, Frances told her sisters, "Be calm, the Lord will change his heart."[2] Sure enough, the next time they met, the cardinal told her to open not one, but two schools: one outside the walls of Porta Pia and another in the Sabine Hills.

After starting multiple schools in Italy, Frances was sure her next step would be the East. However, when she met with Pope Leo XIII, he told her to head west. He had heard from the archbishop of New York of the plight of hundreds of thousands of Italian immigrants, mostly poor peasants, who had moved to the United States. They struggled to find work, their children played in the streets because of the lack of proper schools, and the mortality rate was high since they often had difficulty getting access to hospitals. Consequently, there were many unsheltered orphans. Furthermore, because of the dearth of Italian-speaking priests, the families in the tenements were losing touch with their faith, an integral part of their culture back home.

Disappointed at first, Frances and her sisters nonetheless accepted the assignment. When they arrived in New York, the archbishop tried to send them back. He had been unable to find the right facilities or the funding for them. Frances refused to leave. She traveled New York's Little Italy on foot to minister to the immigrant families and managed to set up an orphanage. For the next twenty-seven years, Mother Frances (as she was then known) traveled back and forth between North America, Europe, and Central and South America, establishing schools, orphanages, and hospitals. By the time she died in 1917, 1,500 women had joined the Missionaries of the Sacred Heart of Jesus with sixty-seven houses of sisters in eight different countries.

If you read a full biography of Mother Frances, you will be struck by how often she was met with challenges that seemed insurmountable. However, her response was always the same. She accepted the seemingly impossible task and set to work doing it immediately, trusting in God to clear up whatever obstacles stood in the way. For example, when she needed a new home for orphans outside New York City, she set her sights on an old mansion that, she was told, did not have a sufficient water supply. Frances insisted it was a gift from God, and within days of taking possession, the sisters found an underground spring on the property.

In 1912, Frances was searching for a building for a new orphanage near Seattle. While she was walking home with some of her sisters, a woman in a limousine offered them a ride back to the convent. That night Frances had a dream of a villa on a hill. The next day, she visited Lake Washington and saw the very same villa. She went up to the house and asked the owner if he'd consider selling—and he turned out to be the husband of the woman in the limo. The house was up for sale, and they were all too happy to sell it to Mother Frances and her sisters.

In the early days of the convent in Codogno, a creditor came to collect on a bill. Frances sent a sister to get the amount from the cashbox, but the sister returned stating there was nothing left. Frances prayed for a moment and then sent her back, saying, "Perhaps you did not look well, look again."[3] When the sister went back to the box, she found the precise amount they needed.

Mother Frances Cabrini's faith got her through these hard times. Rather than seeing her trials as a burden, she saw them as a blessing and often repeated, "Blessed be the day in which it shall be given me to suffer for a cause so holy and pious."[4] Each time she experienced difficulty she put her trust in God and saw it as a sign that the "seal of the cross" had been put on her work.[5]

WHAT CAN WE LEARN FROM ST. FRANCES XAVIER CABRINI?

I have many things in common with St. Frances Xavier Cabrini (short stature, Italian ancestry, vocation as teacher, strong work ethic), but seeing challenges in my life as blessings is not one of them! If an archbishop said to me, "Sorry, I have no money and no place for you to stay, you'd better go back home," I'd probably do it. But that's why Frances is a saint, and I am still a work in progress. Here are some things I've learned from her.

- *Trust in the Lord to bring you what you need.* When asked to start a school, orphanage, or hospital in a new location, Frances would travel to the city and immediately begin searching for the perfect site. She would often decide on buying it before she had the money. She was confident that the Lord would find the necessary funds. If you're struggling with getting some work done and can't see a clear path ahead, keep moving forward and trust the Lord to remove the obstacles as he did for St. Frances.

- *Get out of the way of your own ego.* Once, when the details of a sale couldn't be worked out, Frances left town, sensing that perhaps she was in the way of the Lord's work and trusting that as soon as she left, the matter would be cleared up. She was right! Many people were willing to help Frances in her charitable work because of her humility, but that didn't mean she was always successful. Instead, she willingly stepped aside, trusting the Lord to provide what was needed for the work he had called her to do.

- *Take a break when needed.* With her poor health, Frances often had to be sent away to rest. She would use her boat trips back and forth across the Atlantic as retreat times. In her later years, while working at Columbus Hospital in Chicago, she became ill and was sent to rest in Park Ridge, a suburb that was still quite rural at the time. So much did she benefit from the rest that she bought a vacation home there so that other sisters could take time away. Even if you're a workaholic like me and St. Frances Xavier Cabrini, take time for breaks! Your body, mind, and soul need them.

Appeal to Proper Authorities: St. Mary MacKillop

Mary MacKillop (1842–1909), Australia's first canonized saint, founded the Sisters of St. Joseph of the Sacred Heart, a congregation dedicated to providing free education to the poor. The desire to care for the poor came out of the experience of her own childhood.

Mary Helen MacKillop was born near Melbourne, Australia, to Scottish immigrant parents. Despite her father's good education, he struggled to provide for his wife and eight children. By age fourteen, Mary worked full-time as both a teacher and a governess to help provide for her younger siblings. In 1864, she opened a boarding school for girls in Portland, Victoria, with the help of her friend Fr. Julian Woods. Fr. Woods admired Mary's practical approach as well as her ability to understand the cultural needs of the Indigenous poor in the Australian countryside. With his guidance, Mary started the Sisters of St. Joseph of the Sacred Heart, also known as the Josephites, and opened Australia's first Catholic school.

At first, the sisters were greatly admired for their charity work since Australia had virtually no public assistance for the poor. Bishops like James Quinn in Brisbane invited the sisters to start schools for the poor in their communities. However, friction quickly arose. Mary had her own ideas about how her congregation should be run. She wanted her sisters to own no property. Instead of living in convents, they lived among the people they served. The sisters also held no social distinctions among them; other religious orders had "choir" and "lay" members, but Mary wanted radical equality among her sisters.

Mary also believed strongly that her order should answer to the pope and not be managed by the local bishop. When Bishop Quinn wanted to move the sisters under his diocesan authority and force them to live in a convent, she appealed to Bishop Laurence Sheil of Adelaide. He misunderstood her efforts, thought she was simply being disobedient, and excommunicated her. (How many times have we as educators tried to do what we believe is best for our students only to be misunderstood by someone higher up and then chastised for our efforts?)

Mary was hurt by the accusations against her but accepted the misunderstanding calmly and told her sisters not to criticize the bishop. Instead, she left quietly. Months later, Bishop Sheil repented on his deathbed and removed Mary's excommunication. Mary then headed to Rome to get formal approval of her order's constitution from Pope Pius IX. The process took two years.

When Mary returned to Australia, her troubles continued. The bishop of Adelaide started a rumor that Mary was an alcoholic and had misused the congregation's funds. An official inquiry by Rome exonerated her. Then the Australian bishops united in an attempt to overturn the order's constitution and place it under diocesan control. Once again, Rome came to the rescue and nullified this attempt, stating that the Mother General, not a bishop, would oversee the order. Even so, Mary was removed from her position, and Sr. Bernard Walsh became Mother General. Ten years later, Sr. Bernard died, and Mary became the Mother General once again. Even her friend Fr. Woods came under attack and was removed as spiritual director of the Josephites.

Despite these obstacles, almost 800 women belonged to the order when Mary died, and they ran 117 schools in Australia and New Zealand with more than 12,000 students. In the years to come, the Sisters of St. Joseph, the Sisters of Mercy, and the Christian Brothers founded MacKillop Family Services. Recently, it has come to light that some of the institutions founded by these groups participated in the separation of parents and children. This was not in keeping with Mary MacKillop's desire for the Sisters of St. Joseph to live and work among the poor. MacKillop Family Services has since apologized to the former residents that suffered abuse in some of their institutions.[6]

WHAT CAN WE LEARN FROM ST. MARY MACKILLOP?

If I had been in Mary's position and had a string of arrogant, misguided men trying to mess with my attempts to educate students, I don't think I would have responded as calmly as she did. In the course of twenty-five years in the classroom, I've worked with at least thirteen different principals. Some have been fabulous and created climates of warmth, professionalism, and genuine concern. A few, I'm afraid, had other priorities—like one principal who told us not to disturb her if her door was closed because she was working on her dissertation! And a few just seemed interested in making themselves look good to the outside world so that they could move to the next job.

Working under ineffective administrators can take a toll on a teacher's health. I remember one person in particular made me so anxious that I developed gastritis, which made eating excruciating. I can only imagine what physical ailments I might have developed if I'd been in Mary's shoes.

Perhaps Mary's response can provide us with a road map for handling tough situations, especially those in which others want to tell us how to run our classrooms.

- *Change your perspective.* Mary saw her persecutors as her "most powerful benefactors."[7] Why? She had a similar approach to St. Frances Xavier Cabrini. She saw them as providing her with a cross to bear, and she knew that picking up our cross draws us closer to Christ. I'm not suggesting that we actively seek crosses, but when troubles come upon us, can we view them as opportunities to grow?
- *Avoid gossip.* Mary could have told everyone she knew that the bishops were treating her terribly. Instead, she did not openly criticize the bishops and warned her sisters not to do so as well. This is one of her traits I find most difficult to emulate. There are appropriate times and ways for teachers to speak out against ill treatment of themselves and their students, just as Mary sought the proper authorities in Rome to settle her problems. However, schools, and particularly faculty lounges, can become places of trash-talking others. The next time I'm tempted to gossip or complain in a way that is not productive to improving the school, I hope I remember to ask St. Mary MacKillop to pray for me.

- *Take proper action to rectify an unjust situation and trust that right will win out in the end.* As soon as her excommunication was lifted, Mary took action to solve her order's problem. She headed to Rome to meet with the pope. She knew having her order formally ratified by the pope was the proper way to settle how her congregation would be run.

Saint Squad Summary: Find the Third Path

In his book *The Happiness Advantage*, psychologist Shawn Achor explains how happiness leads to success, not the other way around. According to Achor, study after study has demonstrated that people of all ages and disciplines can rewire their brains to think positively so that they experience better productivity and greater accomplishments.

Achor describes how happy people always find a "Third Path" that leads them to success.[8] Most people, when faced with a difficult situation, see only two paths before them: one leads to negative consequences, while the other maintains the status quo. However, those with a positive mindset look for a Third Path, one that will lead them out of failure and into a time of tremendous growth. Another way to say this is that while some people experience post-traumatic stress or simply try to survive trauma, others experience post-traumatic growth. That doesn't mean seeing the world through rose-colored glasses, but rather seeing trauma and challenges as chances to grow.

The saints in this chapter were experts at finding the Third Path. St. Frances Xavier Cabrini kept looking for money until she found it. St. Mary MacKillop went straight to Rome when her bishops wouldn't help. St. Augustine originally tried finding his own Third Path without God (i.e., moving from town to town in search of better students!), but eventually, he gave in and learned that God is the one who provides the Third Path. These saints knew another path existed because they knew God would never leave them. Their faith in him meant that a window would open whenever a door closed. If the going's getting tough right now, look for your Third Path. Trust in the Lord to light it up for you.

REFLECTION QUESTIONS

1. St. Augustine of Hippo had an accountability partner in St. Jerome. In what ways have your coworkers held you accountable?
2. St. Frances Xavier Cabrini trusted that the Lord would provide her with the means necessary to do her work. How has the Lord provided for your work in unexpected ways?
3. St. Mary MacKillop avoided speaking ill of the bishops who mistreated her. How do you avoid gossip in the workplace and work with proper authorities to resolve issues?

NINE

Saints Who Embraced Lifelong Learning

> The world exerts all its power to gain women, to rob them of their faith and ruin them. Let us however work to train a few [women]. . . . For in this century, we must no longer count on men to preserve the faith.
>
> —St. Madeleine Sophie Barat

Recently, I watched a teacher's TikTok labeled *Every Teacher PD*. The series of short video clips mocks teacher professional development sessions. The guy starts by apologizing for the technology not working, even though it worked "the first time." Then he has everyone come to the front of the room for the sign-up sheet *after* they are all comfortably seated. He swears they'll finish an hour or two early, apologizes for bringing only two dozen donuts for more than one hundred people, and then stops using his microphone. Of course, no one can hear him after that. Finally, he apologizes for going an hour or two longer than he'd expected.

As someone who has offered many professional development sessions for teachers, I laughed at the technology bit because no matter how many adapters I bring, having a technology issue is still my biggest nightmare.

Watching the rest of the TikTok, I began to cringe. Sure, I've sat through some bad PD in my time (we all have), but I've also had some good sessions, where I've walked out with ideas I could use the next day or later in the month. On those occasions when professional development seems like a waste of time, a few saints can help us see the value of being lifelong learners, even if it means looking outside the usual scope of PD.

Keep Loving Language: St. Lawrence of Brindisi

Lawrence of Brindisi, born Giulio Cesare (Julius Caesar) Russo (1559–1619), never worked in a school; however, his preaching was so effective that he is now known as the patron saint of preachers and considered a Doctor of the Church.

Cesare's parents realized while he was young that he had a strong interest in monastic life, so they arranged for him to be educated at the Franciscan monastery in Brindisi, Italy. He entered the Capuchins at age sixteen. His preaching attracted great crowds and converted so many people, including bringing many Lutherans back to the Catholic Church, that Pope Clement VIII called him to Rome to continue his work of evangelization.

In 1596, the pope sent Lawrence to Germany to start new Capuchin houses in an effort to quash heresies in that region. After a year in Germany, he opened houses in Vienna, Prague, and Graz. Around this time, the Turks threatened to invade Hungary as revenge against their defeat at Lepanto. They seemed unstoppable. Carrying only a crucifix, Lawrence marched out in front of the Christian army that went to meet the Turks. Despite being outnumbered, the Christians defeated the invaders.

What was the secret to St. Lawrence of Brindisi's success in so many different countries? Surely, his strong faith and prayer life were vital, but if you dig a little deeper into his life story, you'll learn that he also had an extraordinary gift for languages. He learned to speak at least eight languages, including Latin, Hebrew, and Greek. He mastered these last two languages so that he could study the Bible in its original form. He found that by reading the Bible in the original languages he became a better preacher. So in-depth was his study of scripture that one cardinal claimed Lawrence could recite the Bible from memory!

WHAT CAN WE LEARN FROM ST. LAWRENCE OF BRINDISI?

My great-great-grandfather (an immigrant from a French-speaking area of Switzerland) knew seven languages—almost as many as St. Lawrence of Brindisi. As someone who has struggled with conversational German and Italian, I've always been jealous of him. But my lack of success hasn't kept me from giving up the quest!

Have you or your students been tempted to give up when learning becomes difficult? May St. Lawrence intercede for you when that happens.

- *Know your content area really well.* I'm not saying you need to memorize vast quantities of the Bible like St. Lawrence to be a good teacher (though memorizing scripture is never wasted time). I will say, however, that my work as a writer of both fiction and nonfiction has improved my ability to teach writing. When students ask me questions like why I care about formatting and font size, I can say, "Because if you want to write in the 'real world,' you have to stick to the formatting guidelines your publisher gives you!" Also, I often have discussions with other writers about things like the Oxford comma (I'm pro Oxford comma, for the record), and I think that if you want to talk about Jesus's mom, you should write it as *Jesus's mom* and not *Jesus' mom.* (The *Chicago Manual of Style* and I agree, by the way.) So while you might not need to memorize your content, I do believe that the better we know our content area, the better we will be at teaching it, just as Lawrence improved his preaching by knowing the Bible in multiple languages.

- *Know the "language" of your students.* Speaking of languages, I have no doubt that one of the other reasons Lawrence learned so many languages was so that he could preach effectively in the various countries he visited. As someone who has taught in classrooms where more than a dozen different languages have been represented within a group of twenty-four students, I know that I will never master all of their home languages. However, I make it a point to ask the students questions about their home languages. As a language arts teacher, I can easily fit this into our grammar discussions as I ask them to compare English grammar with the grammar of other languages.

Knowing the "language" of your students can also mean simply listening to them talk. What are the common slang terms they use? What are the cultural references they make? Don't mimic them. (Of course, if you want to make a middle schooler laugh, go ahead and insert the latest catchphrase into your lesson.) What's important here is *knowing* your students.

Return Often to the Well of Wisdom: St. Madeleine Sophie Barat

Ironically, this patron saint of teachers and schoolgirls was homeschooled! Often referred to by her middle name, Madeleine Sophie Barat (1779–1865) grew up in France at a time when girls were generally not educated. However, when her older brother and godfather Louis came home after his training at the seminary to work as a deacon and a schoolmaster, he realized that his ten-year-old sister was exceedingly bright and began teaching her at home. Later, he was ordained a priest, and Sophie's education was effectively interrupted when Louis was imprisoned for two years during the French Revolution. Released in 1795, he brought Sophie to Paris, where he continued her education with lessons on scripture, theology, and the writings of the church fathers.

As the first wave of the revolution died down, new Christian schools were needed. In 1800, a priest named Fr. Joseph Varin asked Sophie to start an association of religious women dedicated to educating girls. He saw this new order as being a counterpart to the Jesuit order, which was focused on educating boys. He believed that God wanted Sophie to lead a life that combined prayer and teaching—and that she would teach her sisters to do the same.

In 1802, Sophie became the superior of the Society of the Sacred Heart, which ended up establishing 105 schools in Europe and sending teams to start schools in America. The order established boarding schools for wealthy girls and used the profits to open day schools for poor girls.

WHAT CAN WE LEARN FROM ST. MADELEINE SOPHIE BARAT?

Sophie wasn't interested solely in the education of the schoolgirls; she was also concerned with the education of her religious sisters (the girls' teachers). As a forward-thinking educator, she insisted that her sisters stay up-to-date with contemporary methods of education so as to know the latest pedagogical techniques. At the same time, she emphasized what was most important, reminding her sisters to "be humble, be simple, and bring joy to others. When Jesus is the reason for your actions, he will act by his Spirit in you."[1]

What can we take away from St. Madeleine Sophie Barat's life and work?

- *Don't be afraid to learn new things.* Sophie encouraged her sisters to try new educational methods. I'd never suggest throwing out something that works for you and your students, but that doesn't mean you can't also be open to something new that might work even better. Some of us are old enough to remember the whole language versus phonics debate. Why some educators threw out phonics entirely while others refused to try incorporating some elements of whole language, I'll never fully understand. We can try new things and still keep the things that work.

- *Keep your eyes on the prize.* Sophie reminded her sisters to keep Jesus at the center of what they did. Sometimes learning new educational technology tools greatly enhances our pedagogy. Other times it seems simply like using technology for technology's sake. Keep your end goal in mind and search for ways your new tools can help you meet that goal.

Don't Wait for Someone Else to Teach You: Sts. Andrew Kim Taegon, Paul Chong Hasang, and Companions

To appreciate the story of Sts. Andrew Kim Taegon, Paul Chong Hasang, and their companions, it is necessary to understand how Catholicism entered their home country of Korea. In 1784, a young Korean scholar named Yi Seung-hun traveled to Peking (Beijing), China, where he was baptized. He then returned to Korea with Catholic books and articles. These sparked interest in Christianity, and his friends and family soon asked to be baptized. Despite the lack of priests in Korea, Christianity spread through the faith of these first Catholics and what they learned from books brought into the country.

Soon the Korean government began persecuting Christians, wanting to rid the country of Western influence. When missionary priests were smuggled in, the government tortured their followers in an effort to find them. Still, the number of Catholic families grew.

One of those families was Paul Chong's. Paul was born around 1794. His father was a Catholic intellectual who was killed after writing the first Catholic catechism in Korean. Undeterred by his father's martyrdom, Paul became a catechist in order to pass on the faith he had learned from his family. He also successfully lobbied Rome to set up a Korean vicariate, which was established in 1831. Although they now had a bishop to help teach the faith, the Korean Catholics suffered from terrible persecution. Often they were tortured, having their limbs twisted until they broke and then beheaded. Paul Chong was among those martyred when he refused to renounce his faith.

One of Paul Chong's contemporaries, Andrew Kim Taegon, became Korea's first ordained priest. Like Yi Seung-hun, he had to travel outside of Korea to learn more about the faith, attending a seminary in the Portuguese colony of Macau before being ordained in Shanghai. He died just a year later as a martyr.

Over the course of one hundred years, approximately 10,000 Christians were martyred in Korea. Among them, 103 were canonized saints. These included 92 laypeople (45 men and 47 women).

WHAT CAN WE LEARN FROM STS. ANDREW KIM TAEGON, PAUL CHONG HASANG, AND COMPANIONS?

Can you imagine becoming a teacher without having any previous teachers of your own—no one after whom you could model your instructional methods, classroom-management style, or assessment techniques? The early catechists in Korea had no catechists to serve as role models. They had to learn entirely on their own what it meant to be teachers of the faith.

- *Sometimes we have to seek out learning opportunities.* The early Korean Christians had no priests or catechists to guide them. They had one man who brought in some books and articles. In a sense, Korea evangelized itself. This wasn't the typical case of missionaries coming in and converting large groups of people; these were people going outside their own country and begging for help from others. Sometimes we have to go outside our own schools and professional learning communities to find the training we need.

- *Pass on what you learn to others.* Imagine if the scholar Yi Seung-hun had never shared his books with others. Imagine if the people closest to him hadn't continued to pass on what they had learned. The Church in Korea never would have expanded. But they did share the faith with others, and the Church grew thanks to their willingness to pass on what they learned. When you pick up a useful tech tool or attend some worthwhile PD, do you share it with your coworkers?

Saint Squad Summary: You're Never Too Old to Learn Something New

In December 2022, a ninety-year-old woman received her college degree from Northern Illinois University, seventy-one years after she started. Joyce DeFauw spent three and a half years at NIU before getting married and starting a family. She became a respected Sunday school teacher and always enjoyed teaching and learning. As the years passed, she admitted to regretting that she never finished her degree. Her children and grandchildren (one of whom was an NIU alumnus) encouraged her to go back to school. So in 2019, her eldest son helped her buy and set up her very first computer. Joyce took her classes online from her retirement home and graduated in 2022.

You might think, *What's the point?* Clearly, Joyce didn't need a college degree anymore. However, in her own words, "It's nice to finish something you started."[2] She admits that it wasn't always easy, but that's how life is. And going back to school just prior to the pandemic had a bonus. When COVID-19 kept family and friends from visiting her in her retirement home, she was already connected online, and her new computer helped her stay in touch with loved ones and classmates. We never know what benefits we may get by keeping an open mind and pursuing the new learning opportunities God puts in front of us.

REFLECTION QUESTIONS

1. St. Lawrence of Brindisi became an expert on scripture so that he could better evangelize. What new area might you study to become a better expert at your content?
2. St. Madeleine Sophie encouraged her sisters to keep up with the latest pedagogical methods. How have you sought out ways to improve your teaching?
3. The early Korean martyrs dedicated themselves to learning about the faith and then sharing that knowledge with others, even at great personal risk. When was the last time you read a good book on teaching and passed it on to someone else who might benefit from it?

TEN

Saints Whose Prayer Lives Kept Them Going

The more intense and visible her external activity,
the deeper and more fervent her interior life must be.
—Bl. Maria Caridad Brader

The words of Bl. Maria Caridad Brader about "intense and visible" external activity really resonated with me the first time I read them. Teaching can be very intense, and it certainly puts us in a very visible position where our work is not only seen by our students, parents, and administrators but also evaluated in formal and informal ways. Therefore, it's wise to take Maria's advice and cultivate a strong interior prayer life. Let's look at some saints whose strong interior lives helped them to be good educators.

Prioritize Spiritual Reading and the Sacraments: St. Elizabeth Ann Seton

Elizabeth Ann Bayley (1774–1821) was born into a wealthy, aristocratic Episcopalian family in New York City. In 1794, she married William Magee Seton, who was also from a prominent family. Elizabeth enjoyed dancing and theater, and she and Will helped plan George Washington's fiftieth birthday party.

Elizabeth and Will were deeply in love and had five children within eight years. Unfortunately, they faced trials as well. Less than four years after they married, Will's father died, so they took charge of Will's seven orphaned half-brothers and sisters. Will also struggled with his business and his health. When he contracted tuberculosis, he and Elizabeth traveled with their eight-year-old daughter Anna to Italy, where Will's business friends, the Filicchis, lived. They hoped the warmer climate would improve Will's health, but the authorities suspected his illness was yellow fever and forced the family to quarantine in a damp, cold building near the sea for almost a month.

During this time, Elizabeth relied heavily on her faith to sustain her. She described the room as having a "brick floor, naked walls, and a jug of water."[1] The noisy wind from the sea sent icy drafts through the prisonlike quarters. To console herself, her husband, and her daughter, she read often from scripture, especially the book of Psalms, and prayed constantly. Elizabeth wrote, "Often when he [William] hears me repeat the Psalms of Triumph in God, and read St. Paul's faith in Christ with my Whole Soul, it so enlivens his Spirit that he also makes them his own, and all our sorrows are turned into joy."[2] When it became too hard for Elizabeth to remain cheerful, she would hide her head in the chair by Will's bed and pray until she could lift her head again.

Eight days after they were released from quarantine, Will died. Elizabeth and her daughter stayed on with Antonio and Amabilia Filicchi, who showed them great compassion and kindness. The Filicchis also introduced Elizabeth to the Catholic faith. She learned the Memorare prayer and fell in love with the Blessed Mother. Elizabeth's own mother had died when she was young, and when her father remarried, her stepmother was often busy with her own children. In Mary, Elizabeth found the mother figure she had been seeking for years.

When she returned to New York, Elizabeth went back to St. Paul Episcopal Church, but her heart was pulled toward the Real Presence in the Eucharist. She wrote to the Filicchis: "I got in a side pew which turned my face towards the Catholic Church [St. Peter's] in the next street, and found myself twenty times speaking to the Blessed Sacrament there . . . tears plenty, and sighs as silent and deep as when I first entered your blessed Church of Annunciation in Florence."[3]

In 1805, Elizabeth joined the Catholic Church. To support her family, she started a school, but when people learned she had converted, they pulled their children out, fearful that she would try to convert them. However, Reverend Louis William Valentine Dubourg, the president of St. Mary's College in Baltimore, invited Elizabeth to start a Catholic school for girls on the campus. In this school, the girls went to the chapel early in the morning and prayed the Rosary and made an examination of conscience in the evening. They studied reading, math, music, grammar, drawing, sewing, and needlepoint. Two young women joined Elizabeth's efforts, and they planned to start a new congregation. A donation from a wealthy convert allowed them to start the first free Catholic school in America.

On March 25, 1809, Elizabeth took her vows as a religious and became "Mother Seton." A few months later, her congregation, the Sisters of Charity of St. Joseph's, was officially founded in Emmitsburg, Maryland, and St. Joseph's Academy opened the next year. Mother Seton made sure to hire competent lay teachers in fields that her sisters were not prepared to teach. She visited the classrooms daily and created such a bond with the students that they would often write to Mother Seton for advice long after graduation.

In order to do the will of God, Elizabeth recommended that one rely on three things: good spiritual reading, prayer, and the sacraments. She told others to do some devotional reading every day and to pray without ceasing.

WHAT CAN WE LEARN FROM ST. ELIZABETH ANN SETON?

As the patron saint of Catholic schools, St. Elizabeth Ann Seton helps us understand how a strong faith life can support us in our work.

- *Let the Blessed Sacrament give you strength.* After her first encounter with the Real Presence in Italy, Elizabeth was drawn to Christ in the Eucharist. She drew strength from this close communion with God. Spend time contemplating how Jesus gives you strength each time you receive the Eucharist.
- *Incorporate spiritual reading into your prayer time.* Teachers don't have much, if any, spare time for reading during the school year. However, I have found that I can make progress if I set small goals, such as a page or two a day. It's not much, but it adds up. Also, there are plenty of devotional books out there with daily passages that can be read in less than five minutes. I give myself a few minutes for spiritual reading in the morning with a cup of coffee or in the afternoon with a cup of tea. I'll set a five- or ten-minute timer on a prayer app and read or pray until the timer goes off. You can also make use of spiritually themed audiobooks and podcasts during your commute to and from school each day.

Spend Time in Adoration: Bl. Maria Caridad Brader

Maria Josefa Karolina Brader (1860–1943) was born in Switzerland and lost her father at an early age. Her widowed mother recognized her daughter's intelligence and made sure Maria received the best education possible.

In 1880, Maria entered a cloistered Franciscan convent and took the name Mary Charity of the Love of the Holy Spirit. She was known as Sr. Caridad and just two years later made her final vows. She began teaching at the convent school and, by the end of that decade, volunteered to be one of six sisters sent to work in Ecuador as a teacher and catechist.

In 1893, Maria was transferred to Colombia and saw the urgent need for more missionaries, so she founded the Franciscan Sisters of Mary Immaculate. She was the superior general of the order from its founding until 1919 and again from 1928 to 1940. She believed her sisters needed to combine contemplation and action. The action part of her plan included making sure that her sisters who worked as teachers also received a good education. She told them "not to forget that the better educated, the greater the skills the educator possesses, the more she will be able to do for our holy religion and the glory of God."[4]

Maria knew, however, that action needed to be balanced with contemplation. To that end, she focused on prayer and spiritual reflection. When faced with an important decision, she made sure to take time in Eucharistic adoration first.

WHAT CAN WE LEARN FROM BL. MARIA CARIDAD BRADER?

The patron of missionaries, teachers, and catechists, Bl. Maria Caridad Brader provides an example of integrating our interior lives with our external work.

- *Find your local adoration chapel and just sit with Jesus.* Maria knew that spending time in Christ's presence would help her be a better teacher. I don't spend nearly as much time sitting quietly in adoration as I should. Twenty years ago, I couldn't even have told you where an adoration chapel in my area was. Over the last ten years, more and more adoration chapels have been added to local churches, but I still have to go a bit out of my way to reach one that's open consistently during the day. When I do find the time to get there, I am rewarded with a sense of peace. No wonder Maria spent time in Eucharistic adoration before making major decisions.

- *Remember that prayer and action go together.* Like St. Frances Xavier Cabrini, Maria loved to spend time in contemplation yet was also a woman of action. Once St. Frances and Bl. Maria spent time in prayer and knew where the Lord was leading them, they set off immediately to get the job done. Is there something in the education field God is calling you to do?

Learn from the Saints: St. Ignatius of Loyola

As someone with education degrees from two Jesuit universities, I've grown quite fond of "Iggy," as my friends sometimes call St. Ignatius. Even though he wasn't a regular classroom educator, I wanted to include him in this book for three important reasons. First, his teachings in the 6,813 letters he left behind have passed on a wealth of knowledge about the Catholic faith. Second, the order he founded (the Jesuits) runs more than 2,300 schools (including twenty-eight colleges and universities) around the world.[5] And finally, Ignatius's own story is also relevant to us, as the course of his life was turned around by the saints. And since that's what we're trying to do here (reorient our own lives by studying the saints), he's worth studying.

As a boy growing up in northern Spain, Ignatius of Loyola (1491–1556) dreamed of being a valiant soldier whom the ladies adored. In fact, it's possible that he was a little too friendly with the ladies and might even have fathered a child as a young man. We do know that he had a police record for getting into a nighttime brawl—not exactly a holy beginning.

In 1521, the course of Ignatius's life changed dramatically when a cannonball hit him during the Battle of Pamplona. He was sent back to Loyola, the family home, to recuperate. His broken leg was not set properly, and he spent the rest of his life with a limp.

As he recuperated, Ignatius looked to books for entertainment, but the only ones that were available to him were religious in nature, especially ones on the lives of the saints. Over time, his dream of being a valiant, dashing soldier transformed into a desire to live a heroic life like the saints he had discovered. His previous dreams of being a soldier and pursuing women left him dry, but dreams of doing great things for God brought him great peace.

Ignatius went to Montserrat, a monastery in Spain, and laid down his knightly armor. After making a good Confession, he dressed in simple pilgrim's clothing and headed to the nearby small town of Manresa. He spent several months praying, fasting, and begging before heading to Jerusalem. There, he realized he needed more education in order to become a priest. Thus, he went to three universities in Alcalá, Salamanca, and Paris. He was so determined to get the proper education that he took Latin classes with small boys when he was thirty years old.

In Paris, Ignatius finished writing *The Spiritual Exercises*, a handbook on prayer and the spiritual life. He taught these exercises to his friend and roommate, Francisco Xavier, the great Jesuit missionary priest. In his Spiritual Exercises, Ignatius laid out a four-week retreat designed to help people grow closer to Jesus, contemplate his life, and understand how to make decisions that align with God's will. Today, Jesuits are required to make this retreat twice in their lives, but laypeople can also do these exercises.

WHAT CAN WE LEARN FROM ST. IGNATIUS OF LOYOLA?

As the patron saint of spiritual retreats, St. Ignatius of Loyola reminds us to take time out of our busy lives to listen carefully to God.

- *To pray well, study the life of Jesus.* The best way to study the life of Jesus is simply to read scripture. Intimidating? Start with the Gospel of Mark; it's the shortest. Feel like you're reading but not fully comprehending or catching the significance of small details? Find a good study Bible that comes with commentary (like the *Living the Word Catholic Women's Bible*, published by Ave Maria Press) or listen to Fr. Mike Schmitz's *Bible in a Year* podcast.

- *Become familiar with consolation and desolation, and use those feelings to help you make decisions as an educator.* I'm a huge fan of going on retreat, especially at Jesuit retreat houses where you can learn more about St. Ignatius, his process of discernment, and how to notice moments of consolation and desolation in your life. Taking time away can be hard during the school year, but there are options for retreats during summer and spring breaks and even online retreats if you need to be home to care for your family. There are also many books about Ignatius's Spiritual Exercises, such as Ave's *The First Spiritual Exercises* (Michael Hansen, SJ) and *Abide in the Heart of Christ* (Joe Laramie, SJ). If you want to dig even deeper, ask your parish priest or Jesuit retreat house to help you find a spiritual director that you can meet with once a month.

- *Keep studying the lives of saints.* When I started this project, I had no idea how many saints were patrons of educators and catechists, and how many saints spent at least part of their time as teachers. Even with the ones included here, I'm only scratching the surface of their biographies. If one or two of them have captured your interest, might I suggest finding more books on them? You may have even more in common with them than you thought. And if you're looking for more new friends to add to your squad, here are a few to check out:

- St. Francis de Sales—This patron saint of both writers and teachers only revealed his desire to become a priest to his father after acquiring his doctorate. As a priest and then a bishop, he made it a priority to educate both the laity and the priests of his diocese.
- Bl. Basil Moreau—This priest and seminary professor founded the Congregation of Holy Cross, which started many schools including the University of Notre Dame. Reading his biography, you will be astounded by the incredible number of hurdles he faced while establishing and expanding his order.
- Mother Angela Gillespie—While visiting her brother at the University of Notre Dame, Angela Gillespie met Fr. Edward Sorin, who convinced her to become a Sister of the Holy Cross. She became the first director of St. Mary's Academy (later St. Mary's College), organized her sisters to serve as nurses during the Civil War, and worked tirelessly for the higher education of women. She also edited the *Ave Maria*, a periodical begun by Fr. Sorin that was the origin of Ave Maria Press.

Saint Squad Summary: Let Scripture and the Saints Be Your Guide

In his apostolic letter *Verbum Domini* (*The Word of God*), Pope Benedict XVI discusses how our personal relationship with Christ is tied to our understanding of scripture: "Thus it is decisive, from the pastoral standpoint, to present the word of God in its capacity to enter into dialogue with the everyday problems which people face."[6]

Does scripture have answers to your teaching dilemmas? I didn't think so . . . until I made a retreat studying the Gospel of Mark, which eventually gave me the idea to write *Sweet Jesus, Is It June Yet?* Jesus was a teacher. Studying his life through scripture can certainly bring us closer to becoming the teachers God is calling us to be.

In the same apostolic letter, Pope Benedict wrote: "The interpretation of sacred Scripture would remain incomplete were it not to include listening to *those who have truly lived the word of God: namely, the saints. . . .* The most profound interpretation of Scripture comes precisely from those who let themselves be shaped by the word of God through listening, reading and assiduous meditation."[7] Go ahead and give yourself a little pat on the back. By reading this book, you are doing exactly what Pope Benedict prescribed. You are reading and meditating on the lives of those who let themselves be shaped by their study of scripture. May their example further our resolve to lead lives of action informed and inspired by contemplation.

REFLECTION QUESTIONS

1. St. Elizabeth Ann Seton knew the benefits of devotional reading, prayer, and the sacraments. How might you make these things a bigger part of your life?
2. Bl. Maria Caridad Brader cherished her quiet time with Jesus. Can you find a local Eucharistic adoration chapel and make time this week to stop by? If yes, put it in your planner or digital calendar. If you schedule it, you're more likely to do it.
3. St. Ignatius of Loyola's life changed when he studied the lives of the saints. How can you continue your study of the saints after reading this book? Is there a local saint's shrine you can visit? If so, then it's time for your own personal field trip—no chaperoning required!

Following Your Vocation Wherever It Leads

The nation doesn't simply need what we have. It
needs what we are.
—St. Teresa Benedicta of the Cross

In the post-pandemic years, an astonishing number of teachers have
left the classroom. Some leave for good; others may return. Some have
chosen careers tangential to education.

Throughout my own career, I've struggled to varying degrees
about my decision to remain in the classroom. If I'm meant to be
a teacher, shouldn't I know that to the very marrow of my bones?
God called me to be a teacher; I'm sure of that. However, there were
times that were so challenging that I considered trying out a whole
new career field. (See *Sweet Jesus, Is It June Yet?* for the time I almost
became a pastry chef.) I earned my doctorate so that I would have
more career options. Should I use this degree to teach future teachers

125

at night while remaining in the middle-school classroom, or do I wait a few more years and make full-time academia my "retirement job"? Imagine my solace in finding saints who struggled with their own decisions about remaining in their profession.

Time to Find a Second Career? St. Teresa Benedicta of the Cross

Born in Breslau, Germany, Edith Stein (1891–1942) was the youngest of eleven children in an Orthodox Jewish family. She was such a bright student that she finished kindergarten at age four. She wore out her teachers to the point that they sent her home and told her parents to keep her home two more years.

Throughout her school years, Edith had high scores in every subject except math. At age thirteen, she gave up her Jewish faith, a decision that broke her mother's heart. In 1911, she began studying at the University of Breslau, only three years after women were first allowed to enter academic institutions in Prussia. For the next two years, she studied philosophy, history, psychology, and German philology. After becoming interested in the work of phenomenologist Edmund Husserl, she transferred to the University of Göttingen, where she befriended Adolf Reinach, Husserl's assistant. When Adolf was killed in World War I, Edith was shocked by how calm his widow Anna seemed. Anna revealed that she relied on her Christian faith to get her through.

Edith's work as a teacher had its share of bumps. She began as a substitute teacher at a secondary school from February through October 1916 while working on her thesis. By August 1916, she had earned her doctorate in philosophy and was soon working as Edmund Husserl's academic assistant. Edith hoped for a position on the university faculty; however, those jobs were not open to women, so she continued to teach in Breslau and tutor privately.

While visiting a friend's house in 1921, Edith saw St. Teresa of Ávila's autobiography on a shelf. She read it in one night and believed that Teresa had written the truth she had been seeking in her work as an academic. The next morning, she bought a Catholic catechism book and began studying it. On New Year's Day in 1922, she was baptized. She wanted to follow in the footsteps of St. Teresa of Ávila and enter the Carmelite monastery, but becoming a Catholic was enough of a shock to her family and a priest advised her to hold off for a while. So she taught at a school in Speyer run by Dominican sisters from 1922 until 1930.

What was Edith like as an educator? By some accounts, she was compassionate and well respected. However, despite her tremendous intellect, she wasn't very good at teaching: "She taught standing motionless, without gestures, speaking in a low monotone, and she made scathing remarks about their work."[1] She sounds a bit like some of my math professors—brilliant at math, terrible at explaining how to do it. At the very least, we know from one of her own letters that she did not really see herself as a teacher: "I do not take myself too seriously as a teacher, and still have to smile when I have to put it down anywhere as my profession."[2]

In 1930, Edith quit her teaching job in Speyer. A priest friend encouraged her to keep writing, and she spent the next two years working on her long treatise *Potency and Act* while maintaining a busy speaking schedule. In 1932, she finally got a position teaching philosophy at the German Institute for Scientific Pedagogy in Münster. However, that only lasted two semesters. In 1933, Hitler came to power in Germany, and all Jewish employees of the state—including teachers—were forced out of their jobs. Edith saw this as a sign that it was finally time to become a Carmelite and entered the monastery in April 1934. Even there, Edith was encouraged by her superiors to keep writing. She left behind a legacy of articles, letters, and translations of Catholic documents.

After the terrible events of *Kristallnacht*, Edith feared her presence would endanger her fellow Carmelites, so she was moved to a Carmelite monastery in the Netherlands. In 1941, Hitler invaded the

Netherlands. Edith Stein and her sister, who had entered the monastery as a Third Order Carmelite, were arrested and sent to a concentration camp. Edith died in a gas chamber at Auschwitz in August 1942.

WHAT CAN WE LEARN FROM ST. TERESA BENEDICTA OF THE CROSS?

Edith Stein didn't plan on teaching at an all-girls school. It was the job she did for many years while waiting to teach philosophy at the university level. After becoming Catholic, she wanted to enter a Carmelite monastery, but it took about eleven years before the timing was right.

- *If God is calling you to move on, listen to him.* When Edith told her Jewish family of her decision to enter the monastery, her siblings tried to dissuade her, mostly for the sake of their mother, who was once again devastated by Edith's choice. Despite the difficult conversations and the tears, Edith wrote that she felt a sense of peace as she took the train away from her family home. She knew in her heart that she had made the right decision. In Ignatian spirituality, this feeling of peace is termed *consolation.* Edith knew she was following God's path for her life.
- *Be open to using your gifts in new ways.* If you are contemplating leaving the classroom, consider whether your alternative plan is providing you with that same sense of peace. Realize, too, that leaving the classroom doesn't have to mean leaving teaching entirely. When she entered the monastery, Edith's superiors insisted she continue writing. The articles and works she left behind became her new way of teaching. Recognizing the brilliance in her writing, her fellow Carmelites hid (even buried underground) many of her compositions during the Holocaust so that they would not be destroyed. If God is calling you elsewhere, consider how he might be asking you to use your talents as a teacher in a new way.

Consider Opportunities Education-Adjacent: Bl. Marie-Léonie Paradis

Virginie-Alodie Paradis (1840–1912) was born in Quebec, Canada. At age fourteen, she entered the Marianites of Holy Cross convent in Saint-Laurent, Montreal. The Marianites are a women's religious order associated with the Congregation of Holy Cross. Marie-Léonie taught in and around Montreal until 1862, when she moved to New York to work at the St. Vincent de Paul orphanage.

In 1870, Marie-Léonie moved to the American community of the Holy Cross sisters in Indiana, where she taught French and needlework at St. Mary's Academy. In the fall of 1874, she returned to Canada to take charge of the sisters who did domestic work at St. Joseph's College in New Brunswick. She felt called to serve Jesus through his priests; six years later, she founded the Little Sisters of the Holy Family. Their mission was to assist the priests of the Congregation of Holy Cross in their education work.

WHAT CAN WE LEARN FROM BL. MARIE-LÉONIE PARADIS?

- *Consider serving those who teach.* I don't know what Bl. Marie-Léonie was like as a teacher or whether she enjoyed teaching French and needlework. However, it's clear she felt called to assist priests who also worked in education. If you feel God is calling you out of the classroom but you still care deeply about the profession, perhaps he wants you to serve those in education. I've known educators who have left the classroom but taken jobs for academic book publishers, online learning programs, and teacher-training programs.

Redeem Retirement: Bl. Mary Kevin

Teresa Kearney (1875–1957) was born in County Wicklow, Ireland. Her dad died before she was born, and her mother died when Teresa was only ten. At age fourteen, she became a teacher for the Sisters of Mercy at Rathdrum. Three years later, her grandmother died, and she moved to Essex to teach school there. It was at this assignment that she had a dream, for three nights in a row, that she was working for dark-skinned people who needed her assistance.

This dream was fulfilled in 1889, when Teresa took vows as Sr. Mary Kevin for the Franciscan Sisters of St. Mary's Abbey in Mill Hill, London. Their mission was to work with people of African descent. In 1902, Sr. Mary volunteered to work in Uganda. Having no teaching supplies, she used the sandy ground for a blackboard. She trained African women as nurses and founded high schools and a teacher-training college. One of her main goals was to empower African women through education. She taught the first East African women to serve in the legislature, earn bachelor's degrees, and become doctors.

In her late seventies, Sr. Mary "retired" to work as the superior of a convent in Boston, where she raised funds for African missions. Despite living away from Africa during her final years, she was so beloved by the Ugandans that when she passed, they raised funds to have her remains brought from Ireland back to Uganda. To this day, to perform a *kevina* in Uganda is to perform some act of great generosity.

WHAT CAN WE LEARN FROM BL. MARY KEVIN?

• *Retirement doesn't mean you have to give up your passion for education.* When I was student teaching at a middle school, my supervising teacher was a woman who went by the name "Miss U." She never married, and teaching had been her whole life. She retired as soon as I finished my student teaching. Here I was at the very beginning of my career, and she was at the end of her thirty-plus years in the field. One day, she said, "I've been 'Miss U' for over thirty years. Who am I going to be now?" Her whole identity was wrapped up in being an educator. She couldn't imagine who she would become.

By the time this book is published, I will probably have fewer than ten years left in a regular classroom. My contemporaries and I have had numerous conversations about when we'll retire and what we'll do next.

What I admire about Bl. Mary Kevin is that even in her retirement, she found a way to be involved in education by raising funds for African schools. If you're retiring soon, and you're worried about losing your identity as an educator, ask the intercession of Bl. Mary Kevin, who found a way to contribute, just in a different way than she had anticipated.

What's Next

Only God knows what tomorrow will bring. As I look toward my final years in the classroom, I consider my options. With my doctorate, I could certainly work as an adjunct professor. Perhaps I will continue writing books and leading retreats for educators, hoping they'll inspire the younger ones to hang in there. After all, we need great educators!

But the truth is that I simply don't know where God will call me next. If I've learned anything from my saint squad, it's that our God is a God of surprises. He exalts the lowly. He humbles those in authority. He gives us dreams and then either helps us fulfill them or replaces them with completely new ones.

I'm grateful for the members of my saint squad, who have helped me throughout this book-writing process. I've asked for their prayers constantly in my teaching as well. If a student is being challenging, I ask St. John Bosco and St. Jean-Baptiste de La Salle to pray for me. If I feel like I'm losing my joy, I ask Bl. Thea Bowman to shout out to the Lord for me. If I need courage to persevere, I ask St. Frances Xavier Cabrini and St. Elizabeth Ann Seton to remind me of God's undying faithfulness. I hope you've come to see these friends as your own saint squad, too.

I started this book with a quote from St. Philip Neri, and I will end it with one. As you walk this path to sainthood with your squad at your side, may this thought bring you comfort and courage.

> Cast yourself with confidence into the arms of God.
> And be very sure of this, that if he wants anything
> of you, he will fit you for your work and give you
> strength to do it.
>
> —St. Philip Neri

INTRODUCTION

1. Samantha Smylie, "New Survey Shows Illinois Schools Find It Difficult to Find Qualified Teachers," Chalkbeat Chicago, February 2, 2023, https://chicago.chalkbeat.org.

2. John Schmitt and Katherine deCourcy, "The Pandemic Has Exacerbated a Long-Standing National Shortage of Teachers," Economic Policy Institute, December 6, 2022, https://www.epi.org/publication/shortage-of-teachers/. Italics in the original.

1. SAINTS WHO USED RELATABLE AND CREATIVE TEACHING TECHNIQUES

1. Linda Darling-Hammond, *The Right to Learn: A Blueprint for Creating Schools That Work* (San Francisco: Jossey-Bass, 1997), 170.

2. Maurice J. Nutt, *Thea Bowman* (Collegeville, MN: Liturgical Press, 2019), 5–6.

3. Nutt, *Thea Bowman*, 86.

4. Blake Britton, "Antonio Cuipa and Companions," Word on Fire, May 14, 2019, https://www.wordonfire.org/articles/antonio-cuipa-and-companions/.

5. Bert Ghezzi, *Voices of the Saints: A Year of Readings* (New York: Doubleday, 2000), 608.

6. Ghezzi, *Voices*, 592.

7. Daughters of St. Paul, *In Caelo et in Terra: 365 Days with the Saints* (Boston: Pauline Books & Media, 2020), 254.

8. Quoted in *Catechism of the Catholic Church* (New York: Doubleday, 1995), 14.

2. SAINTS WHO BUILT STRONG RELATIONSHIPS

1. Catherine of Siena, *The Dialogue* (Huntington, IN: Our Sunday Visitor, 2019), xiv.

2. Catherine of Siena, *The Dialogue*, xi.

3. Ghezzi, *Voices*, 649.

4. Religious of the Assumption, "St Marie Eugenie of Jesus," 2019, http://www.assumptionreligious.org/about-us/st-marie-eugenie.html.

5. Religious of the Assumption, "St Marie Eugenie of Jesus."

6. Religious of the Assumption, "St Marie Eugenie of Jesus."

3. SAINTS WHO DEALT WITH CHALLENGING STUDENTS

1. Susan H. Swetnam, *My Best Teachers Were Saints* (Chicago: Loyola Press, 2006), 23.

2. Ann Ball, *Modern Saints: Their Lives and Faces*, Book One (Charlotte, NC: Tan Books, 1983), 102.

3. Augustin Auffray, *How St. John Bosco Punished*, trans. Peadar Walsh (Dickinson, TX: Te Deum Press, a Division of Angelus Press, 2020), 19–20.

4. George Van Grieken, *The Teacher's Saint: Saint John Baptist de La Salle, Patron Saint of Teachers* (Washington, DC: Christian Brothers Conference, 2019), 79, ebook.

5. Van Grieken, *The Teacher's Saint*, 22.

6. Van Grieken, *The Teacher's Saint*, 23.

4. SAINTS WHO ADVOCATED FOR CHANGE

1. Vatican News Services, "Marie-Anne Blondin (1809–1890)," accessed January 8, 2023, https://www.vatican.va/news_services/liturgy/saints/ns_lit_doc_20010429_blondin_en.html.

2. Vatican News Services, "Marie-Anne Blondin (1809–1890)."

3. Sr. Joan Gormley, "Saint John of Avila and the Reform of the Priesthood," Catholic Culture, April 2004, https://www.catholicculture.org/culture/library/view.cfm?id=6038.

5. SAINTS WHO SOUGHT JUSTICE FOR THEIR STUDENTS

1. Rachel Bulman, "A Chapter That Changed My Life: 'Love and Responsibility,'" Word on Fire, September 7, 2020, https://www.wordonfire.org/articles/a-chapter-that-changed-my-life-love-and-responsibility/.

2. Xavier University of Louisiana, "The Life and Legacy of Our Foundress: Saint Katharine Drexel," March 3, 2020, https://www.xula.edu/news/2020/03/the-life-and-legacy-of-our-foundress-saint-katharine-drexel.html.

3. Peter Stockland, "Search for Truth over Graves Is Elusive," *The Catholic Register*, September 7, 2023, https://www.catholicregister.org/item/35846-search-for-truth-over-graves-is-elusive.

4. Red Cloud Indian School, "Ground Penetrating Radar," https://www.redcloudschool.org/pages/our-story/history/ground-penetrating-radar.

5. Gregory Boyle, *The Whole Language: The Power of Extravagant Tenderness* (New York: Avid Reader Press/Simon & Schuster, Inc., 2021), xvi.

6. SAINTS WHO SURPASSED EXPECTATIONS

1. Ghezzi, *Voices*, 694.

2. Ghezzi, *Voices*, 30.

3. Ball, *Modern Saints*, Book One, 336.

4. James Martin, *My Life with the Saints* (Chicago: Loyola Press, 2016), 129.

5. Ball, *Modern Saints*, Book One, 73.

6. Amy J. Heineke, *Restrictive Language Policy in Practice: English Learners in Arizona* (Bristol, UK: Multilingual Matters, 2017), 204.

7. SAINTS WHO TAUGHT IN TIMES OF CRISIS

1. Ball, *Modern Saints*, Book One, 298–99.

2. Ball, *Modern Saints*, Book One, 302.

3. Meg Hunter-Kilmer, *Pray for Us: 75 Saints Who Sinned, Suffered, and Struggled on Their Way to Holiness* (Notre Dame, IN: Ave Maria Press, 2021), 54.

8. SAINTS WHO KEPT GOING WHEN THE GOING GOT TOUGH

1. Mitch Finley, *The Seeker's Guide to Saints* (Chicago: Loyola Press, 2000), 55.

2. Segundo Galilea, *In Weakness, Strength: The Life and Missionary Activity of Saint Frances Xavier Cabrini* (Quezon City, Philippines: Claretian Communications, 1996), 50.

3. Galilea, *In Weakness, Strength*, 45.

4. Galilea, *In Weakness, Strength*, 78.

5. Galilea, *In Weakness, Strength*, 110.

6. MacKillop Family Services, "Apology to Former Residents," accessed April 2, 2023, https://www.mackillop.org.au/about-mackillop/our-history/apology-to-former-residents.

7. Robert Ellsberg, *All Saints: Daily Reflections on Saints, Prophets, and Witnesses for Our Time* (New York: Crossroad, 1997), 337.

8. Shawn Achor, *The Happiness Advantage: How a Positive Brain Fuels Success in Work and Life* (New York: Currency, 2018), 108.

9. SAINTS WHO EMBRACED LIFELONG LEARNING

1. Daughters of St. Paul, *In Caelo et in Terra*, 150.

2. Sara Smart, "71 Years after Starting College, a 90-Year-Old Woman Is Graduating," CNN, December 11, 2022, https://www.cnn.com/2022/12/11/us/90-year-old-woman-graduates-college-trnd/index.html.

10. SAINTS WHOSE PRAYER LIVES KEPT THEM GOING

1. Anne Merwin, *Elizabeth Ann Seton* (Boston: Pauline Books & Media, 2015), 27.

2. Merwin, *Elizabeth Ann Seton*, 27.

3. Merwin, *Elizabeth Ann Seton*, 38.

4. Catholic News Agency, "Blessed Maria Caridad Brader," accessed October 24, 2022, https://www.catholicnewsagency.com/saint/blessed-maria-caridad-brader-160.

5. Society of Jesus (Jesuits), "Education," accessed January 29, 2023. https://www.jesuits.global/ministries/education/.

6. Benedict XVI, *Verbum Domini: Post-Synodal Apostolic Exhortation on the Word of God in the Life and Mission of the Church*, September 8, 2010, para. 23, https://www.vatican.va.

7. Benedict XVI, *Verbum Domini*, para. 48.

EPILOGUE: FOLLOWING YOUR VOCATION WHEREVER IT LEADS

1. Swetnam, *My Best Teachers Were Saints*, 172.

2. María Ruiz Scaperlanda, *Edith Stein: The Life and Legacy of St. Teresa Benedicta of the Cross* (Manchester, NH: Sophia Institute Press, 2017), 85.

Bibliography

Achor, Shawn. *The Happiness Advantage: How a Positive Brain Fuels Success in Work and Life.* New York: Currency, 2018.

Auffray, Augustin. *How St. John Bosco Punished.* Translated by Peadar Walsh. Dickinson, TX: Te Deum Press, a Division of Angelus Press, 2020.

Ball, Ann. *Modern Saints: Their Lives and Faces.* Book One. Charlotte, NC: Tan Books, 1983.

———. *Modern Saints: Their Lives and Faces.* Book Two. Charlotte, NC: TAN Books, 1991.

Benedict XVI. *Verbum Domini: Post-Synodal Apostolic Exhortation on the Word of God in the Life and Mission of the Church.* September 30, 2010. www.vatican.va.

Blessed Is She. "Friends with Saints Series: Natalia Tulasiewicz." August 1, 2020. https://blessedisshe.net/blog/friends-saints-series-natalia-tulasiewicz/.

Boyle, Gregory. *Whole Language.* New York: Avid Reader Press/Simon & Schuster, Inc., 2021.

Britton, Blake. "Antonio Cuipa and Companions." Word on Fire. May 14, 2019. https://www.wordonfire.org/articles/antonio-cuipa-and-companions/.

Bulman, Rachel. "A Chapter That Changed My Life: 'Love and Responsibility.'" Word on Fire. September 7, 2020. https://www.wordonfire.org/articles/a-chapter-that-changed-my-life-love-and-responsibility/.

Butler, Alban. *The Lives of the Saints.* Charlotte, NC: TAN Publishers, 1955.

Catechism of the Catholic Church. New York: Doubleday, 1995.

Catherine of Siena. *The Dialogue.* Huntington, IN: Our Sunday Visitor, 2019.

Catholic News Agency. "Blessed Maria Caridad Brader." Accessed October 24, 2022. https://www.catholicnewsagency.com/saint/blessed-maria-caridad-brader-160.

Catholic Online. "St. Philip Neri." Accessed November 8, 2023. https://www.catholic.org/saints/saint.php?saint_id=97.

Centre Marie-Léonie Paradis. "Mother Marie-Leonie Paradis." 2020. https://
www.centremarie-leonieparadis.com/en/mere-marie-leonie/.

Costello, Damian, and Jon M. Sweeney. "Black Elk, the Lakota Medicine
Man Turned Catholic Teacher, Is Promoted for Sainthood." *America*.
October 1, 2017. https://www.americamagazine.org.

Côté, Louise. "Marguerite Bourgeoys and Respect for Creation." Congréga-
tion de Notre-Dame. April 19, 2016. http://cnd-m.org/en/news/article.
php?id=1275.

Darling-Hammond, Linda. *The Right to Learn: A Blueprint for Creating
Schools That Work*. San Francisco: Jossey-Bass, 1997.

Daughters of St. Paul. *In Caelo et in Terra: 365 Days with the Saints*. Boston:
Pauline Books & Media, 2020.

DelFra, Lou, and Ann Primus Berends, eds. *5 Minutes with the Saints: More
Spiritual Nourishment for Busy Teachers*. Notre Dame, IN: Ave Maria
Press, 2014.

De Maria, Saverio. *Mother Frances Xavier Cabrini*. Translated by Rose Basile
Green. Turin, Italy: Società Editrice Internazionale, 1984.

Diocese of Rapid City. "Black Elk Documentary." Black Elk Canonization website. 2021. https://blackelkcanonization.com/
black-elk-documentary/.

———. "Walking the Good Red Road: Nicholas Black Elk's Journey to Sainthood." Vimeo. May 19, 2020. https://vimeo.com/420363725.

Ellsberg, Robert. *All Saints: Daily Reflections on Saints, Prophets, and Witnesses for Our Time*. New York: Crossroad, 1997.

Finley, Mitch. *The Seeker's Guide to Saints*. Chicago: Loyola Press, 2000.

Galilea, Segundo. *In Weakness, Strength: The Life and Missionary Activity
of Saint Frances Xavier Cabrini*. Quezon City, Philippines: Claretian
Communications, 1996.

Ghezzi, Bert. *Voices of the Saints: A Year of Readings*. New York: Doubleday,
2000.

Gormley, Sr. Joan. "Saint John of Avila and the Reform of the Priesthood."
Catholic Culture. April 2004. https://www.catholicculture.org/culture/
library/view.cfm?id=6038.

Greek Orthodox Archdiocese of America. "Dorotheus, Abba of Gaza."
Accessed August 28, 2022. https://www.goarch.org/chapel/
saints?contentid=2217.

Guiley, Rosemary Ellen. *The Quotable Saint*. New York: Facts on File, 2002.

Hallig, Marc Jozsef Lester. "Commemoration of Blessed Natalia Tułasiewicz." Philippine Carmelites. March 21, 2022. https://carmelitesph.org/commemoration-of-blessed-natalia-tulasiewicz/.

Heerey, Frances. *Biographies: God at Their Sides*. New York: Regina Press, 1984.

Heineke, Amy J. *Restrictive Language Policy in Practice: English Learners in Arizona*. Bristol, UK: Multilingual Matters, 2017.

Heinlein, Michael R., ed. *Black Catholics on the Road to Sainthood*. Huntington, IN: Our Sunday Visitor, 2020.

Hunter-Kilmer, Meg. *Pray for Us: 75 Saints Who Sinned, Suffered, and Struggled on Their Way to Holiness*. Notre Dame, IN: Ave Maria Press, 2021.

Johnson, Maria Morera. *Super Girls and Halos: My Companions on the Quest for Truth, Justice, and Heroic Virtue*. Notre Dame, IN: Ave Maria Press, 2017.

Linehan, Dennis M. "Explainer: Who Was Mother Katharine Drexel, the Second American-Born Saint?" *America*. September 16, 2000. https://www.americamagazine.org/issue/380/article/mother-katharine.

MacKillop Family Services. "Apology to Former Residents." Accessed April 2, 2023. https://www.mackillop.org.au/about-mackillop/our-history/apology-to-former-residents.

Martin, James. "The Feast of St. Katharine Drexel." *America*. March 3, 2011. https://www.americamagazine.org.

———. *My Life with the Saints*. Chicago: Loyola Press, 2016.

Merwin, Anne. *Elizabeth Ann Seton*. Boston: Pauline Books & Media, 2015.

"Natalia Tułasiewicz." Wikipedia. February 18, 2022. https://en.wikipedia.org/wiki/Natalia_Tu%C5%82asiewicz.

Nutt, Maurice J. *Thea Bowman*. Collegeville, MN: Liturgical Press, 2019.

O'Driscoll, Mary. *Catherine of Siena*. Strasbourg, France: Editions du Signe, 1994.

Orthodox Church in America. "Venerable Abba Dorotheus of Palestine." Accessed August 28, 2022. https://www.oca.org/saints/lives/0216/06/05/101628-venerable-abba-dorotheus-of-palestine.

Pramuk, Christopher. "The Witness of Sister Thea Bowman." *America*. June 24, 2014. https://www.americamagazine.org.

Religious of the Assumption. "St Marie Eugenie of Jesus." 2019. http://www.assumptionreligious.org/about-us/st-marie-eugenie.html.

Scaperlanda, María Ruiz. *Edith Stein: The Life and Legacy of St. Teresa Benedicta of the Cross*. Manchester, NH: Sophia Institute Press, 2017.

Schmitt, John, and Katherine deCourcy. "The Pandemic Has Exacerbated a Long-Standing National Shortage of Teachers." Economic Policy Institute. December 6, 2022. https://www.epi.org/publication/shortage-of-teachers/.

Simeone, Renato. "Blessed Peter To Rot." Catholic News Agency. January 25, 1995. https://www.catholicnewsagency.com/resource/55604/blessed-peter-to-rot.

Sisters of Notre Dame of Chardon, Ohio. *Saints and Feast Days: A Resource and Activity Book*. Chicago: Loyola Press, 2006.

Smart, Sara. "71 Years after Starting College, a 90-Year-Old Woman Is Graduating." *CNN*. December 11, 2022. https://www.cnn.com/2022/12/11/us/90-year-old-woman-graduates-college-trnd/index.html.

Smylie, Samantha. "New Survey Shows Illinois Schools Find It Difficult to Find Qualified Teachers." Chalkbeat Chicago. February 2, 2023. https://chicago.chalkbeat.org.

Society of Jesus (Jesuits). "Education." Accessed January 29, 2023. https://www.jesuits.global/ministries/education/.

Swetnam, Susan H. *My Best Teachers Were Saints*. Chicago: Loyola Press, 2006.

Van Grieken, George. *The Teacher's Saint: Saint John Baptist de La Salle, Patron Saint of Teachers*. Washington, DC: Christian Brothers Conference, 2019.

Vatican News Services. "Marie-Anne Blondin (1809–1890)." Accessed January 8, 2023. https://www.vatican.va/news_services/liturgy/saints/ns_lit_doc_20010429_blondin_en.html.

Xavier University of Louisiana. "The Life and Legacy of Our Foundress: Saint Katharine Drexel." March 3, 2020. https://www.xula.edu/news/2020/03/the-life-and-legacy-of-our-foundress-saint-katharine-drexel.html.

Amy J. Cattapan is a middle-school English teacher and Catholic speaker, retreat leader, and author who has written or contributed to several books, including *Sweet Jesus, Is It June Yet?*, *Chicken Soup for the Soul: From Lemons to Lemonade*, and the award-winning novels *Angelhood* and *Seven Riddles to Nowhere*. She hosts *Cath-Lit Live!* for the Catholic Writers Guild.

Cattapan has appeared on *The Katie McGrady Show* on SiriusXM, EWTN's *Bookmark*, *Catholic Faith Network Live*, and the *Son Rise Morning Show*. Her writing has appeared in *Highlights for Children*, *Hopscotch for Girls*, *Pockets*, and *Catechist*. She also served as the host for Shalom World TV's *BOOK.ed*.

Cattapan earned a bachelor's degree in English secondary education from Marquette University, a master's degree in instruction for secondary education language arts from Northeastern Illinois University, and a doctorate in curriculum and instruction from Loyola University Chicago. She has spoken at a variety of conferences, including NCEA, the Los Angeles Religious Education Congress, and C3.

She lives in the Chicago area.

www.ajcattapan.com
Facebook: acattapan
Twitter: @AJcattapan
Instagram: @a.j.cattapan
Pinterest: @ajcattapan
YouTube: A.J. Cattapan

ALSO BY
AMY J. CATTAPAN

Sweet Jesus, Is it June Yet?

10 Ways the Gospels Can Help You Combat Teacher Burnout and Rediscover Your Passion for Teaching

You work hard to motivate your students every day, but where can you find the inspiration you need when teaching gets tough or your passion for the classroom starts to wane?

Amy J. Cattapan invites you to look to the greatest teacher of all time—Jesus. With humor and stories from the trenches, Cattapan draws valuable insight and tools from the Gospels and shares ten life-changing principles every teacher can learn from Jesus. In *Sweet Jesus, Is It June Yet?*, she'll help you hang onto your sanity and fulfill your calling even when you're feeling stressed, overwhelmed, and on the verge of burnout.

In order to combat frustration and burnout, Cattapan will help you:

- remember where your calling began;
- rediscover who this is all about;
- know when to lean on others for help;
- learn how Jesus dealt with challenges; and
- understand that God's grace really is enough.